Cooking for
Celiacs, Colitis, Crohn's & IBS

www.ccccibs.com

Published first in 2007, second in 2008, third in 2009, fourth in 2011
by Elephant Publishing Pty Ltd
www.elephantpublishing.com

Elephant Publishing Pty Ltd
P.O. Box 1820
Noosaville Qld 4566
Phone: 0407 428 481
E-mail: sandra@elephantpublishing.com

Chief Executive: Sandra Ramacher
Publishing Director: Randolph Lagerway

Photographer: Sandra Ramacher
Food Preparation: Sandra Ramacher

Recipes developed by Sandra Ramacher

National Library of Australia Cataloguing-in-Publication Data
Elephant Publishing Pty Ltd.
Healing Foods — Cooking for Celiacs, Colitis, Crohn's and IBS

Bibliography.
Includes Index
ISBN 9780980382808 (pbk.)

1. Gluten-free diet - Recipes 2. Colon (Anatomy) - Disease - Diet Therapy. I. Title

641.56318

Printed in China

IMPORTANT: This book contains recipes which are based on a diet which is to enhance health. The author recognizes that the treatment of illness and the enhancement of health through diet should be supervised by a duly qualified physician. Consult your doctor before starting the diet as proposed here. This book will be of particular help if used in conjunction with the advice of a physician who is particularly specialized in the field of nutrition.

The author and publisher do not assume medical or legal liability for the use or misuse of the information and diet regimen contained in this book.

Those who might be at risk from the effects of salmonella poisoning (the elderly, pregnant women, young children and those suffering from immune deficiency diseases) should consult their doctor with any concerns about eating raw eggs.

*SCD and Specific Carbohydrate Diet are trademarks of Kirkton Press Limited

Cooking for
Celiacs, Colitis, Crohn's & IBS

200+ Specific Carbohydrate Diet™ Recipes

Totally Grain Free, Gluten Free, Sugar Free, and Lactose Free

Elephant Publishing

Contents

Preface

Background

In 1998 I was diagnosed with Ulcerative Colitis. I remember that I had been feeling quite unwell - feverish, tired, faint and suffering urgent bowel movements. After undergoing a colonoscopy I was diagnosed with severe Ulcerative Colitis. I spent years researching the disease and trying all kinds of medication and diets.

Discovering SCD™*

It was not until 2004 that I finally arrived at Elaine Gottshall's website supporting her groundbreaking book *Breaking The Vicious Cycle*. I was amazed at the reviews and worldwide acceptance of Elaine's findings. Judging by the massive raves on the internet, her Specific Carbohydrate Diet had a great success rate. By that time, I was quite anaemic and extremely nervous about going out in public with uncertain proximity to public toilets.

I started the diet immediately, carefully heeding Elaine's warning to follow it on the strictest basis, starting solely with the chicken soup and jelly for the first three days. I built my yogurt maker out of a polystyrene box and 40W lamp, then carefully measured the starter yogurt, heated the milk, poured the mix into jars and nervously waited 24 hours for my first batch to be completed. It tasted great! (I now have a dedicated cupboard in the kitchen with a small built-in lamp with wall switch.)

Progress!

My body reacted immediately. My bowels stopped bleeding after just three days. I carefully progressed to other recipes from Elaine's book for the next 7 days, then followed on with more recipes from the internet and have not looked back since! I still occasionally display minor symptoms such as gas and urgency, but only if I have eaten something that doesn't agree with me - 'legal' or not 'legal' - but definitely not for me. Dried apricots (legal ones), for example, send me running. So I stay away from them. I learned to listen to my body like a piano tuner listens for the wrong note. Then one sunny day in April 2006 my body hit the right note. I had reduced my medication and was taking the absolute minimum amount. I finally took my last pill and haven't taken one since. There is still a packet in the medicine cabinet, untouched for a long time, as a safety blanket.

Medical Advice

A necessary disclaimer is that you MUST seek medical advice before you give up your medication. When I broached the idea of stopping medication my gastroenterologist gave me a very concerned look, quoting statistics that showed inevitably the disease would reoccur. She felt my remission from the disease was thanks solely to the drugs (She had not heard of the SCD diet.) She suggested I take the drugs for the rest of my life. I chose to go against her advice, as the health risks from the drugs were too great to ignore. My symptoms had been gone for over three months and I felt quite confident. My commitment to sticking to the diet on the strictest basis was by then very resolute. I was dreaming up some wonderful SCD recipes and was learning ways to incorporate the diet into my social life. I have been off medication now for over a year.

*SCD and Specific Carbohydrate Diet are trademarks of Kirkton Press Limited

SCD Home and Away

I have learned to be a very humble 'pain in the ...' at restaurants. I generally scan the menus for the most likely meals to be 'improved' upon and explain apologetically to the waiter, that I have a "quite severe allergy" toward certain ingredients in foods. At the very worst I order a piece of fish or meat without the dressing and ask them to swap the inevitable potatoes with something else. A lot of sugar goes into savory foods in restaurants, so I have learned to ask the waiter to check with the chef. Another little eccentric thing I do is take a small container of my homemade Caesar Dressing with me and order a Caesar Salad without the croutons and dressing. I then sneak the dressing on when nobody is looking. It also gets lathered onto the fish or meat. I just love my really tasty condiments and it makes eating out something to look forward to.

Emergency Supplies

My Chewy Date & Macadamia Biscuits, Toffees, or Cheddar Crackers are constant companions, for enjoyment as a dessert or deployment as emergency fuel. Sometimes when I'm away from home and I've forgotten to take something to snack with me, I am amazed that I cannot find anything quick to eat that hasn't got bread wrapped around it. I have bought a sandwich, discarded the bread, only to find a thin slice of cheese, one piece of lettuce and a sad looking sliver of tomato. Not enough to survive on.

Friends and the Diet

My family has no problem with my diet. They eat what I eat. I'm the cook so they don't get a choice when they eat at home. There has never been a complaint and everyone has their favorites. I have made the sticky date pudding so many times now that I could make it blindfolded! The ice-cream is my son's absolute favorite and HE can make that blindfolded. My friends all have a collection of my recipes and make them for their families, even though they do not suffer from any digestive diseases.

The two things I miss the most on this diet is chocolate and ... well... chocolate. There is no substitute for this. So I remind myself that the taste is short lived and it rots your teeth and makes you fat. Actually it's the worst foods that I sometimes crave, just like an ex smoker craves a cigarette. Potato Fries, Pizza, Croissants. When you look at the foods you cannot have on this diet, it's really all the foods that aren't all that good for you anyway. I am in my 40s now and if I was allowed to eat anything I wanted I would be as big as a house. So this diet has become a lifestyle for me. I exercise on a regular basis, I eat great food and I am healthier than ever.

One final point I would like to make about the SCD Diet, is that it is very easy to follow. In comparison to weight loss diets it's an absolute cinch. I have read that one of the major complaints from people on this diet is that it is 'too difficult' to follow. I think you will find that once you have made yourself familiar with my cookbook, cooking for the SCD Diet will become as easy as any other way of cooking. In addition, again I would like to urge you to read Elaine Gottschall's book *Breaking the Vicious Cycle*, as it is essential you begin with the introductory diet, before you progress onto *Cooking for Celiacs, Colitis, Crohn's and IBS*.

Sandra

IMPORTANT NOTICE TO THE READER

It is important to understand that dried fruit and legumes used in these recipes are considered advanced foods, according to the Specific Carbohydrate Diet. A good reference to determine which foods are suitable for each stage of the diet can be found on www.pecanbread.com

Furthermore, it is important to eat all foods in moderation. Just because you found a food that you love, overindulging can cause adverse symptoms.

Each person has individual food sensitivities and therefore it is advisable to exercise caution when introducing a new food to your diet.

Lactose free essentially means that cheeses and yogurt products have to contain less than 1% lactose to qualify as legal foods for the Specific Carbohydrate Diet. Elaine Gottschall recommended some dairy products, such as lactose free milk, are not to be used. Lactose is a milk sugar and is a double molecule. Well fermented milk products such as yogurts and natural cheeses are lactose free — as processes of fermentation the sugar is consumed by the bacteria.

Those suffering from severe intestinal disorders are strongly advised to adhere to the introductory diet outlined in *Breaking The Vicious Cycle* prior to using the recipes in this book.

Introduction

Every recipe in this cookbook is totally grain free, gluten free, sugar free, and lactose free. The book also features many delicious vegetarian dishes. Written specifically for people suffering from bowel diseases like Colitis, Crohn's and IBS, this cookbook also addresses the issues affecting those with gluten intolerance.

All recipes are based on a list of foods compiled by Elaine Gottschall, who pioneered intestinal and neurological health through consumption of the right kinds of carbohydrates. At 47 she earned degrees in biology, nutritional biochemistry and cellular biology, as part of her research. The diet has also shown improvement in the neurological health of autistic children. Please refer to the reference guide at the back of the book or visit our website **www.CCCCIBS.com** for links to the related websites and forums on this diet.

Cooking for Celiacs, Colitis, Crohn's, and IBS provides you with over 200 recipes and over 100 beautiful full color photographs of delicious and easily prepared meals. The recipes embrace every aspect of our daily eating requirements and many have officially received kids' thumbs up awards! You name it, we have it. Mouth-watering desserts, cakes and crispy breads; loads of outstanding main dishes and in between snacks, beverages and some great breakfast ideas.

This book makes the diet as mainstream as possible. We provide you with a weekly and monthly cooking guide to make your life easier. Once you have a stockpile of essential ingredients such as tomato sauce, dripped yogurt and condiments, it's easy to whip up a dinner when you only have half an hour. I can guarantee your taste buds will be delighted and you will never miss ordinary food again.

A shopping guide covers all essential kitchen utensils and ingredients. Purchasing links are provided on our website to help the SCD newcomer.

This book will be most helpful to those of you who are already familiar with Elaine Gottschall's diet and wish to maintain your intestinal health. However, even those not afflicted with intestinal problems have enjoyed the alternate, healthier ways of eating shared in this book. Those wanting to start with the SCD diet should first read Elaine's book, start with the first stages of her diet and then progress to *Cooking for Celiacs, Colitis, Crohn's and IBS*. Your body will love you for it!

Foreword

It is with great pleasure that I provide this introduction to *Cooking for Celiacs, Colitis, Crohn's and IBS*. My perspective is that of a physician with nearly twenty years of experience applying the Specific Carbohydrate Diet (SCD) to a wide range of patients with challenging medical problems. As I sometimes explain to patients who are at first daunted by the food exclusions the diet entails, "Anyone can read about this diet—I'm here to attest that it works!"

Unintentionally, I have become the physician of last resort for myriad patients with bewildering and challenging medical problems. These include many sufferers who either obtain no relief from conventional treatments, or else can't stand the side effects of conventional treatments. Others simply desire a natural way to circumvent the potential side effects of conventional drugs.

For people with serious gastrointestinal maladies, I frequently offer this simple analogy:
If a plumber is summoned to your home to unclog a toilet, he will warn you to desist from throwing pipe-clogging detritus into it. But almost uniformly, conventional gastroenterologists miss the boat by not promoting the food connection to alimentary woes. This reinforces patients' nihilism about the potential role diet might play in resolving their problems.

The analogy to a simple pipe or conduit is overly simplistic, however. Would that the GI tract were only a simple PVC pipe! Thanks to the insights of Elaine Gottschall and subsequent decades of thoughtful research on the role intestinal flora play in the origin of GI diseases, a more complex picture has emerged: We literally carry within us a complex community of organisms which outnumber the cells in our bodies.

These diverse bacteria interact with one another and send signals to the immune cells which line our intestines. They manufacture good and bad chemicals that pass into our bloodstreams and create messages that either suppress or trigger disease.

Why does the balanced ecology of the intestinal tract go awry? Modern life poses many perils to GI normalcy: lack of breast-feeding prevents natural priming of the intestines with "good bacteria" and protective immune substances present in mothers' milk; early childhood diseases prompt indiscriminate use of antibiotics which kill natural flora and give rise to pathogenic species like Candida albicans .

Then the Western Diet takes over. Introduction of evolutionarily-new, domesticated and potentially allergenic foods like wheat, dairy, peanuts, potatoes and corn early in life sets up food allergies. Processed starches and enormous amounts of sugar provide the perfect culture medium for proliferation of harmful bacteria and yeasts. Chlorinated and fluoridated water devastate the gut. And harmful chemical additives and medications like aspirin and NSAIDs inflame and abrade the intestinal walls. Stress and sedentary lifestyle then play havoc with our elimination. To borrow the apt term coined by Elaine Gottschall, a "Vicious Cycle" has now set in, and, for many, disease is the inevitable consequence.

How then to "Break the Vicious Cycle"? Logically enough, one vogue in GI medicine is to use powerful antimicrobial drugs which provide temporary and partial relief to some sufferers, but unfortunately bacteria mutate to become resistant. It has even recently become popular in some "innovative" GI circles to use antibiotics to treat, not just serious diseases like ulcerative colitis and Crohn's Disease, but even irritable bowel syndrome. IBS has earned a disease designation with the advent of new, patentable drugs to treat it.

But it was Elaine Gottshall's genius to envision a different, more natural, and ultimately more permanent way to "Break the Vicious Cycle." This is accomplished via implementation of a diet free of fermentable carbohydrates which give rise to the overgrowth of pathogenic bacteria—the SCD. The experiences of many of my patients attest to its efficacy.

I was fortunate to hear of this diet through an esteemed colleague, Dr. Leo Galland, who learned about it from one of his patients. After trying it with patients, I soon became an enthusiastic advocate and began recommending it to my patients and to listeners of my radio program, Health Talk. Thus began a long collaboration with Elaine Gottschall during which she appeared frequently as a guest on my show, and I was honored to provide an introduction to her book in 1994. In 2005, I was interviewed for a Wall Street Journal article about the SCD.

What kind of patients have benefited from the SCD? In my experience patients with ulcerative colitis or proctitis and Crohn's Disease are prime candidates. So are patients with celiac disease whose GI tracts remain ravaged despite careful implementation of a gluten-free diet. Additionally, many patients with frequent bouts of diverticulitis become symptom-free.

Patients with short-gut syndrome after GI surgery often improve. So do the many women and men who suffer GI symptoms after radiation enteritis caused by treatment for gynecological or urological cancer. Many patients with pouchitis report improvement with the diet.

Finally, while the diet may represent too extreme a commitment for some patients with mild IBS, for those whose lives are seriously impaired it can be a godsend.

What is often surprising to patients is the degree to which they obtain relief from systemic or extra-intestinal manifestations of their disease: energy improves, brain-fog dissipates, headaches disappear, acne and inflamed skin resolve, and joints and muscles stop aching. This attests to the gut origin of some of these seemingly remote complaints.

I sometimes marvel at the ability of young children and teenagers to adhere to a diet which is somewhat constricting and socially ostracizing. But apparently, with the proper family support, and new delicious recipes, the substantial relief they experience motivates them to stick to it.

A caveat: The diet doesn't work for everyone. One reason is compliance: for some the regime is challenging, and without proper resources like Elaine Gottschall's book, the excellent web support now in place, or sympathetic and knowledgeable physicians and nutritionists to fine-tune the diet and encourage compliance, and books like *Cooking for Celiacs, Colitis, Crohn's and IBS* some patients do not adhere to the diet long enough to experience its benefits. Ultimately, there are some patients who may obtain only partial or no amelioration with the diet.

I usually explain to these non-responders that, just as you can't put out a raging fire merely by apprehending the arsonist who has torched a building, so, too, diet alone may not suffice in very case and it may take suppressive medicine to control a disease that has gained considerable momentum. Since many cases of inflammatory bowel syndrome do not respond even to the latest medications, facilitating the body's response to drugs with a therapeutic diet still makes sense, even if improvement is partial.

The popularity of the SCD is a testament to patient empowerment. There's a grass-roots movement underway in medicine, and it is enlightened laypersons like Elaine Gottschall and the authors of *Cooking for Celiacs, Colitis, Crohn's and IBS* who are leading the charge. Let us look forward to the day when more of the medical profession will embrace the SCD as a powerful tool in our arsenal against disease. Meanwhile, take charge of your condition, and bon apetit!!

Ronald L. Hoffman, M.D.
Hoffman Center
776 6th Avenue, Suite 4B
New York, New York
10001

www.DrHoffman.com

July, 2007

Essential Ingredients

Reading Labels on Foods

Elaine Gottschall cautions that "Reading labels, although a good policy, is inadequate for those on the SCD since one ingredient sometimes has numerous names and may not be easily recognized as a forbidden carbohydrate. Many cans, jars, bottles, and packages do not list all ingredients because of different labeling laws in different parts of the country/world. It is recommended that nothing be eaten other than those foods listed in Chapter 9 of *Breaking the Vicious Cycle* and listed as 'Legal' on the 'Legal / Illegal' list. The law also states that any ingredient which is less than 2% of the total volume does not have to be declared. Sugar is one of those ingredients. If you really want to know what is in a product, ring the manufacturer and tell them you have severe allergies to wheat, sugar, starches etc. and they will have to tell what is really in the product.

The foundation of the Specific Carbohydrate Diet is built on restricting the types of carbohydrates ingested. Foods that comply with the diet can be found in the extensive list in the *Breaking The Vicious Cycle* book and website. You can find a link to this list on our website **www.CCCCIBS.com**

Cooking for Celiacs, Colitis, Crohn's and IBS provides you with recipes for all the condiments you need to cook the delicious meals contained in this book.

Here is a list of essential ingredients, which are necessary for the recipes in this book. Check our website **www.CCCCIBS.com** for a comprehensive up to date list of suppliers.

Almond Flour	Almond flour or Almond Meal is frequently used as a substitute for wheat flour in SCD recipes, and can be purchased in bulk at various wholesalers. I buy mine in 10kg boxes. Keep a supply in the fridge in an airtight container and store the rest in the freezer.
Bananas	Bananas need to be ripe, to the point of brown spots appearing on the skin. This is an important consideration when consuming bananas, as the riper the banana the less starch is present.
Baking soda	Also known as bicarbonate soda. It is used instead of baking powder, which contains starch and is illegal on the food list.
Cheese	Most cheeses are allowed, such as cheddar, brie, havarti and parmesan. Refer to the legal/illegal list to check specific cheeses. Processed cheeses and fresh cheeses, such as cottage cheese, feta, mozzarella or ricotta are to be avoided.
Coconut Milk	Elaine recommends making your own coconut milk and does not recommend canned as it contains gums and stabilizers. To make your own follow the Almond Milk recipe on page 241 and substitute almond flour for unsweetened coconut flour.
Coconut	Shredded or flaked coconut needs to be unsweetened. This can usually be purchased from a healthfood supplier.
Dried Fruit	Dried fruits such as dates, apricots, raisins etc must all be untreated. Health food retailers sell organic untreated fruits. The other option is to buy or build a food dehydrator and dry fruit yourself.
Dried Beans and Legumes	It is important that dried beans and legumes be soaked overnight, rinsed, and cooked for their appropriate time (up to 2 hours).

Fish Sauce	Most fish sauces contain sugar. There are a number of manufacturers, who do produce pure fish sauce without sugar. Otherwise, substitute one anchovy fillet per teaspoon of fish sauce used in the recipe.
Grape Juice	Grape Juice needs to be 100% pure. In North America pure grape juice is produced by Just Juice, Welch's and Kedem Kosher Organic Grape Juice. Do not use frozen juice concentrate.
Honey	Honey is a key ingredient in desserts and even in some of the main dishes. A light colored honey is best, as it will have the most neutral flavor. Honey needs to be clear and 100% pure, watch out for honey which has been adulteratd with corn syrup or other sugar solutions.
Green/Red peppers	Also known as capsicum or cayenne peppers.
Nut Butters	Most health food retailers will sell pure nut butters, such as peanut butter, cashew butter or macadamia butter. It is essential that these butters do not contain any added sugar. It is advisable to be careful with roasted cashew butter as sometimes starches are added.
Nuts	Nuts sold in mixed nut mixtures are not allowed as most are coated with a starchy coating. Buy separately and preferably organic.
Oil	Olive oil and grapeseed oil or sunflower oil are some of the healthiest oils to use in cooking. For deep frying use grapeseed oil or sunflower oil. Also use grapeseed oil or sunflower oil for making mayonnaise as olive oil is too heavy and rich in flavor.
Vanilla Essence	Vanilla Essence can be purchased at health food suppliers. It is important that it is sugar free.
Vinegar	White & Red Wine Vinegar needs to be sugar and starch free. The same goes for Apple Cider Vinegar.
Wine	White and red wine needs to be sugar free, so that means it has to be extra dry wine. The sweeter the wine the higher the sugar content. In North America the wines are graded by sweetness with '0' being the driest.
Yogurt Starter	Check our website for buying yogurt starter in your country. A popular option is to purchase additive-free natural commercial yogurt as a starter. Elaine Gottschall advises: "Yogurt starter contains cultures of bacteria that we use to inoculate the milk and begin the fermentation. The bacteria that we should have in our yogurt starters are: Lactobacillus bulgaricus Streptococcus thermophilus. Lactobacillus acidophilus (optional). In fact, without the first two strains above we can't really call it yogurt. The strain we must avoid in our SCD yogurt is Bifidus as it has been found to cause bacterial overgrowth in the gut. Bifidus comes in quite a few variations e.g. Bifidbacterium infantis, Bifidbacterium bifidum, Lactobacillus Bifidus, Bifidbacterium longum etc, in general avoid anything that has bifid in its name. Some yogurt that we use as a starter can contain sucrose, cream, and lactose however; these are consumed in the 24hr fermentation."

Essential Tools

1 Liter/1 Qt. Glass Jars	You will need these jars to make your yogurt and French Cream. You will also need them to store your homemade condiments. Remembering that 250 ml or one cup of yogurt makes one smoothie. So for a family of four you will need seven jars to make enough yogurt for smoothies for one week. It's worth setting aside one day per month to catch up on all condiment cooking. Making the yogurt and French Cream should be done once per week.
Electric Food Processor	This household appliance is an absolute essential for making smoothies, sauces, baking and mashing vegetables. It is also very handy if there are attachments which can grate cheese and carrots, and also interchangeable blades for chopping and mixing.
Electric Hand Mixer	Makes whipping egg whites much easier.
Food Dehydrator	Not essential, but some recipes call for a food dehydrator. This is not an expensive item, but produces great snack. (For children in particular!)
Garlic Press	To get the most flavor out of garlic it needs to be minced finely and this gem will do that in a flash.
Garnish Magic™	This little magic machine turns your zucchinis into endless spaghetti and makes great garnish out of carrots. Check the reference guide at the back of the book for purchasing information.
Measuring cups & spoons	The recipes are given in metric and imperial units. It is easy to use either, but you will need a weigh scale for the metric.
Muffin Tins & Baking Tins	Some of the recipes require small muffin tins and large muffin tins. Breads and cakes will require various baking tins. The main ones needed are small 24 hole muffin tin, large 6 hole muffin tin, 10 x 21 cm/4 x 8 inch loaf tin, 20 cm/8 inch square baking tin. 23 cm/9 inch round tin.
Pyrex Dish	23 x 33 cm/9 x13 inch glass Pyrex dish
Ramekins	These are essential for some of the scrumptious dessert recipes
Slow Cooker	This is not absolutely essential, but it makes making stocks and stews very easy.
Utensils	Spatulas. It is good to have two spatulas for safe flipping; one spatula on top and the other to help flip. Sharp knifes, strainers, mixing spoons, large bowls, cutting boards, etc.
Vegetable Peeler	This little miracle worker is one of my most used kitchen tools. I use it for peeling pumpkins as well as tomatoes, carrots, apples etc.
Waxed Baking Paper	This is essential for any baking recipes in this cookbook. Baking Paper is also known as Cooking Parchment.

Weekly Cooking Plan

The weekly cooking plan is a list of the basic recipes you will need to prepare to ensure your meal planning for the week goes as smoothly as possible. I allocate a few hours every Sunday to make fresh batches so they are available for the next week. They have a shelf life of about 7 - 14 days.

It is also a good idea to plan your meals for the week. Visit our website www.CCCCIBS.com to download our 'Weekly Cooking Planner'. Plan your meals for the week and create a shopping list at the same time! You can also see at a glance which ingredients will need to be prepared in advance.

Yogurt	Each person can easily consume at least a cup of SCD yogurt per day. Considering that the Every Morning Smoothie is so delicious that everyone in the family will want one, and that quite a few of the recipes call for the yogurt as an ingredient, it is wise to make a week's supply.
French Cream	Depending on the desserts and main courses planned for the week, you will need to make enough for all the recipes.
Stewed Apples & Apple and Pear Sauce	I always make a batch of this, as we have it on pancakes frequently and my son takes some for lunch at school.
Raspberry Cordial & Lemonade	Cannot live without it! My son's friends think it's way better than anything in the stores. We mix them with soda water.
Crackers, Bread & Muffins	The pumpernickel bread keeps the best and toasts up great. Since it is a heavy bread I slice it thinly. One loaf usually lasts the whole week. I also make a batch of Cheddar Crackers, but I have to hide them from the rest of the family, otherwise they are gone in minutes. These are great for taking to the movies for munching when everyone else is having potato chips.

I also usually bake some muffins or biscuits, to have with morning or afternoon tea.

If I feel energetic, I make some onion rolls and freeze them for later. Defrost in the oven at 150°C for about 15 minutes.

Monthly Cooking Plan

This is the biggie. One day of cooking, once a month. (Or two half days.) This is what makes the diet exciting and delicious! It mainly includes condiments which are easily stored for 30 days in your fridge. You will need to learn how to store foods properly including sterilizing jars and freezing ingredients in batches.

Stocks	There are three kinds of stock recipes in the book – Chicken, Beef, and Vegetable. Chicken stock can usually be substituted for beef or vegetable so if you are not vegetarian, feel free to just make chicken stock. I make stock over a two-day period in my slow cooker, once every two or three months. I freeze the stock in 500 ml/16 fl oz and 1 liter/1 ¾-pint lots.
Chutneys & Salsas	The chutneys easily last up to 3 months in the refrigerator. It is important to use sterilized jars if making more than one jar at a time. The salsa takes no time at all, so I usually only make it as needed.
Jams	I usually prepare one kilo at a time. This amount does not always last us the month, but it is so easy to make if you run out during the month. Again, it is important to use sterilized jars if making more than one jar at a time.
Tomato Paste & Puree	These are two of the most used essential ingredients in the book. Freeze the paste in small batches, as often only 1 or 2 tablespoons at a time is needed. Try freezing in an ice-cube tray! The puree can also be stored in sterilized jars for up to 3 months or frozen in 500 ml/16 fl oz batches.
Ice Cream	Usually best made weekly, but can also be made monthly.
Sweet Snacks	It does not matter how many sweet snacks you prepare as part of your monthly ritual, they always seem to run out early! Great for children's school lunches or to take on trips. Warning: Beware of the Pecan Toffees. They are addictive.
Sun-dried Tomatoes	I love these on my 'Crusty Onion Roll' sandwiches, so I make a large batch.

Once you have all this in storage, your SCD cooking will be a piece of cake. It can be a challenge to cook for a large family, but I guarantee that if you are well prepared, creating the meals in this cookbook will be easy. No need to cook separate food for different family members any longer. Everyone loves this food!

Yogurt

In the beginning making yogurt can seem quite daunting, but after your first couple of batches it will become quite easy.

1. Heat the milk to 80°C/180°F, which is about as hot as it would get before it starts to boil. Be careful not to boil the milk, especially the goat's milk.

2. Let the milk cool to room temperature. I whisk it occasionally, which stops the skin from forming on top of the milk.

3. Mix in the appropriate amount of yogurt, or yogurt starter. It is vital you read our section on yogurt starter in the Essential Ingredients List. There are also a huge number of links on our website **www. ccccibs.com** which will answer any other questions you might have about SCD and making the yogurt. Elaine Gottschall's book **Breaking the Vicious Cycle** also provides all the essential information needed.

4. The easiest and cheapest way to ferment your yogurt is to use a rigid foam box with a lid. My first yogurt maker was made from this. I used a small table lamp with a 40 W light bulb, which kept the box at just the right temperature. In winter, when temperatures are lower I find I have to increase my light bulb to 60 W. I now have a dedicated cupboard, which has an electrical switch and a light bulb fitting. It is worth acquiring a cooking thermometer to begin with and to measure the temperature of the container to make sure the temperature is around 43 - 45°C/100 - 110°F.

5. Ferment the yogurt for a minimum of 24 hours. It is okay to leave it longer, but the yogurt will become more tart.

6. The yogurt needs to set in the refrigerator for at least 8 hours before using.

Yogurt

Makes 1 Liter (2 cups)

1 ltr (4 cups) milk
60 g (¼ cup) natural yogurt

Purchase a natural yogurt or appropriate starter to make this yogurt. (See the section on essential ingredients for advice, or our reference list at the back of the book). Heat the milk in a medium sized pot. Do not boil. The milk should be around 80°C/180°F Turn off the heat and let the milk cool until you can dip your finger into the milk, which is about room temperature (20 - 25°C/64 - 77°F). Whisk in the yogurt and pour into a screw top jar. Store for 24 hours minimum in a warm place, which will keep the temperature of the yogurt at 45°C.

Refrigerate in an airtight jar for up to two weeks.

Goat's Milk Yogurt

Makes 1 Liter (2 cups)

1 ltr (4 cups) goat's milk
60 g (¼ cup) natural goat's yogurt

Purchase a natural goat's yogurt or appropriate starter to make this yogurt. Heat the goat's milk in a medium sized pot. Do not boil. The milk should be around 80°C/180°F. Turn off the heat and let the milk cool until you can dip your finger into the milk, which is about room temperature (20 - 25°C/64 - 77°F). Whisk in the goat's yogurt and pour into a screw top jar. Store for 24 hours minimum in a warm place, which will keep the temperature of the yogurt at 45°C.

Refrigerate in an airtight jar for up to two weeks.

Goat's Cheese

Makes 1Liter (2 cups)

1 ltr (4 cups) scd goat's milk yogurt^

To make the goat's cheese^, line a sieve with 4 layers of kitchen cloth or cheesecloth. Pour the goat's yogurt into the cloth lined sieve and cover. Let sit in a cool place for 48 hours, after which gather the cloth at the loose ends and squeeze as much fluid out of the cheese as possible. Do this gently. Loosen the cheese off from the cloth and place in an airtight jar and store in the refrigerator.

Refrigerate in an airtight jar for up to two weeks.

^All SCD yogurt items to be as per our home-made recipes.

Dripped Yogurt

Makes 2 cups

1 ltr (4 cups) scd yogurt^

To make the dripped yogurt, line a sieve with 4 layers of kitchen cloth or cheesecloth. Pour the yogurt into the cloth lined sieve and cover. Let sit in a cool place for 24 hours, after which gather the cloth at the loose ends and squeeze as much fluid out of the cheese as possible. Do this gently. Loosen the cheese off from the cloth and place in an airtight jar and store in the refrigerator.

Refrigerate in an airtight jar for up to two weeks.

Labna (Yogurt Balls)

Makes 20

1 liter (4 cups) scd yogurt^
pinch salt
375 ml (1 ½ cups) light virgin olive oil

Place a large colander or sieve over a deep bowl. Place four layers of cheesecloth or any kind of cloth, which is good for draining the yogurt, into the sieve. Pour the yogurt into the cloth and cover. Leave yogurt to drain for 24 hours. No need to refrigerate, but leave it in a cool place. After 24 hours, wrap the cloth over the yogurt. Place a weight, such as a pot filled with fruit, e.g. lemons, onto the yogurt and leave for another 24 hours. Remove pot and gently squeeze as much fluid out of the Labna by tightening the cloth. The Labna is now ready to be rolled into small balls and placed inside a jar filled with light virgin olive oil and pinch of salt. Add herbs, garlic, and peppercorns into the oil if you wish to flavor the Labna. Store in the refrigerator. The oil will set hard when stored in the refrigerator. Remove the jar ½ hour before use to let the oil thin, remove desired quantity, then refrigerate again.
Refrigerate in an airtight jar for up to two weeks.

French Cream

Makes 740 ml (3 cups)

620 ml (2 ½ cups) heavy cream
120 g (½ cup) natural yogurt

Pour cream into a saucepan and over medium heat bring to just short before boiling. Do not let boil. Turn heat off and let cool until you can touch it with your finger (about 45°C/110°F). Mix in the yogurt and pour into a glass jar, tighten lid and place inside a cupboard with a 40 watt light for 24 hours. Make sure the light is placed away from the jar and doesn't shine directly onto it. After 24 hours remove the jar gently from the cupboard and refrigerate for at least 8 hours.
Refrigerate in an airtight jar for up to two weeks.

Appetizers and Snacks

Roasted Tomatoes with Goat's Cheese

Serves 4

6 fresh plum tomatoes – halved
1 Tbs olive oil
salt and pepper
50 g (¼ cup) scd goat's cheese^
1 tsp honey
1 Tbs fresh basil – minced
1 Tbs fresh basil – shredded

Preheat the oven to 170°C/340°F
Line a baking tray with baking paper

Place the halved tomatoes onto the baking tray with inside facing up. Brush with olive oil and sprinkle with salt and pepper. Bake in the oven for 2 hours, until they start to resemble semi sun-dried tomatoes. Remove from the oven and let cool completely. Combine the goat's cheese with the honey and the minced basil. Distribute the cheese onto the semi dried tomato halves and garnish with the shredded basil.

Cheese and Tomato Toasties

Serves 2

1 serving of soft souffle bread*
cheddar – sliced
1 plum tomato

***see page 223 for recipe**

Preheat the grill to 180°C/340°F
Line a baking tray with baking paper.

Make the soufflé bread and cut it in half. Place the cheddar and tomatoes on one-half and place both parts of the soufflé bread onto the prepared baking tray. Grill for a few minutes, until the cheese starts to melt. Remove from grill and place the top half of the soufflé bread onto the filled part. Serve warm.

Chicken and Cauliflower Croquettes

Serves 4

60 g (½ cup) onions - chopped
500 g (1 lb) chicken - minced
200 g (1 cup) cauliflower
1 tsp fresh thyme
½ tsp salt
½ tsp pepper
2 eggs
50 g (½ cup) parmesan cheese - grated
100 g (1 cup) almond flour
80 ml (⅓ cup) olive oil

Sauté onions in a small amount of olive oil until tender. Add the minced chicken and cook about 20 minutes at low temperature until all the moisture has evaporated. Meanwhile, boil 500ml/2 cups of salted water and cook the cauliflower until just soft (about 8 minutes). Drain and place into a food processor with the chicken mince, chopped onion, thyme, salt, pepper and 1 egg and blend until smooth. Refrigerate the mixture for 30 minutes.

Grate the parmesan cheese, mix with the almond flour, and spread onto a large flat plate. Whip the remaining egg in a bowl until light and fluffy.

Take the chicken mixture from the refrigerator. Form into 16, 2 ½ cm x 5 cm/1 x 2 inch croquettes. Dip them into the beaten egg and roll in the almond flour and parmesan mixture until well covered. Heat the olive oil in a non-stick pan and fry croquettes, turning them frequently until golden brown. Place them onto a double layer of kitchen paper towels to remove excess oil. Serve warm with our BBQ sauce and dijonnaise.

Cream Cheese Dip

Makes 370 g (1 ½) cups

330 g (1 ⅓ cup) scd dripped yogurt^
1 fresh plum tomato- chopped
60 g (½ cup) onion - chopped
1 clove garlic - minced
pinch cayenne
salt and crushed black pepper

Place all the ingredients into a food processor and blend until smooth. Season to taste and refrigerate for 2 hours before serving.

Chicken Liver Paté

Makes 3 cups

350 g (11 oz) chicken livers
50 g (2 oz) butter
2 shallots – finely chopped
Salt and pepper
50 ml (2 fl oz) bourbon
2 eggs
80 g (⅓ cup) scd french cream^

Preheat the oven to 150°C/300°F

With a sharp knife remove the veins and fat from the chicken livers. Melt the butter in a medium sized non-stick pan and add the shallots, frying them for about 2 minutes. Then add the chicken livers, salt, pepper, and sauté for another 5 minutes. Pour in the bourbon, deglaze the pan (this means to sauté until any meat residue comes off from the bottom of the pan). Take off the heat, place into a food processor with the eggs and process until smooth. Add the french cream^ and combine. Taste to adjust seasoning and then pour evenly into ramekins. Place the ramekins into a deep baking tray and fill with water until it reaches half way up the ramekins. Place in the oven and bake for 30 minutes. Let cool completely and then refrigerate to set for at least 4 hours. To store, cover with plastic wrap and keep refrigerated.

Pecan and Pea Paté

Makes 3 cups

120 g (1 cup) onions – finely chopped
1 Tbs butter
120 g (1 cup) ground pecans
180 g (1 cup) frozen baby peas
3 eggs – hard boiled
2 cloves garlic – minced
2 tsp fresh dill
80 g (⅓ cup) scd french cream^
salt and pepper to taste

Sauté the onions with the butter until soft and translucent. Add the peas, cover and sauté on low until peas are cooked. Place all the ingredients, except for the french cream into a food processor and process until smooth. Add the french cream^, salt and pepper to taste and blend by hand. Pour into ramekins and refrigerate for at least 4 hours.

To store, cover with plastic wrap and keep refrigerated.

Tri-Bites

Makes about 35

125 g (1 ¼ cup) cheddar – grated
100 g (1 cup) almond flour
60 g (¼ cup) scd dripped yogurt^
½ tsp dried sage
½ tsp dried thyme
¼ tsp cayenne pepper
coarse salt

Preheat oven to 150°C/300°F
Line a baking tray with baking paper

Combine the cheddar with the almond flour, yogurt^, sage, thyme, and cayenne pepper and knead until all ingredients are combined. Place the dough onto the lined baking tray. Place another layer of baking paper on top of the dough. Then roll the dough between the two layers out until about 2mm/¹/₁₆ inch thick. Remove the top layer of baking paper. Press the coarse salt sparingly into the dough. Then with the edge of a knife score the dough diagonally cutting diamond shapes into the dough. Bake in the oven for 15 minutes or until slightly browned. Turn off the oven and remove the crackers. Cut into diamond shapes along the scored lines. Place back into the cooling oven and let sit until oven is completely cooled off. Store in an airtight container.

Pumpkin and Leek Pies

Makes 6

150 g (1 cup) fresh pumpkin - diced
1 ½ Tbs butter
150 g (¾ cup) leeks - chopped
1 Tbs honey
1 clove garlic - minced
10 Eggs
30 g (⅓ cup) parmesan cheese - grated
80 ml (⅓ cup) scd french cream^
salt and pepper

Preheat oven to 180°C/360°F
Lightly oil a large 6-hole muffin tin

Dice pumpkin into 1 cm/½ inch pieces, place in pot, cover and steam in a small amount of water about 10 minutes until they start to soften. Drain and set aside. Heat the butter in a small skillet and add the chopped leeks. Stir and sauté about 2 minutes - until the leeks start to wilt. Add the honey and garlic, and cook, stirring for 3 - 4 minutes. Remove from heat and set aside. In a large bowl combine the eggs, parmesan and french cream^, and mix well. Add the pumpkin and leeks, and season to taste. Pour the mixture into the prepared muffin tin and bake for 30 - 40 minutes until the tops of the pies feel firm. Remove from the oven and let cool for a few minutes before removing from the moulds. Serve at room temperature or cold. Refrigerate in an airtight container.

Fish Dumplings with Green Chili Sambal

Serves 4

400 g (13 oz) firm white fish - minced
100 g (1 cup) peanuts - crushed
3 shallots - finely chopped
10 g (¼ cup) fresh coriander
- finely chopped
60 ml (¼ cup) fish sauce*
2 Tbs honey
1 birdseye chili - minced
oil for deep frying

*see essential ingredients list

Lightly toast the peanuts in a dry skillet. Place all the ingredients into a food processor and combine well. Take about 1 Tbs of the mixture and form into balls. Heat enough oil in a medium skillet or wok to cover the balls when deep-frying. When oil is hot, place the balls onto a metal slotted spoon, immerse into the hot oil, and fry until golden brown all over. Place onto some scrunched up kitchen towel to remove excess oil.

Serve with the green chili sambal.

Green Chili Sambal

4 large green chilies - seeded
and finely sliced
2 shallots - finely sliced
1 small Granny Smith apple - peeled,
cored and finely chopped
3 Tbs fresh coriander - chopped
2 Tbs white wine vinegar
2 Tbs honey
3 Tbs fish sauce*
3 Tbs peanut oil

*see essential ingredients list

Combine all the ingredients in an electric food processor and process until finely chopped. Refrigerate in an airtight container.

Gado Gado

Serves 6

4 medium zucchinis - ends cut
4 medium carrots - peeled
1 red peppers - seeded
150 g (5 oz) green beans - ends cut
1 tsp olive oil

Cut zucchinis and carrots in half, and then cut each half into three pieces. Cut red peppers into half, then quarter and half again.

Place the carrots into a vegetable steamer or cover with hot water in a saucepan. Simmer for 5 minutes, and then place the zucchinis and beans into the water or steamer and simmer for another 5 minutes. The vegetables should be starting to soften, but still be firm. Place the oil into a small saucepan and sauté the red peppers pieces until softened, being careful not to brown them. Cool the vegetables and then arrange them on a serving platter. Serve with the peanut sauce.

Peanut Sauce 1

Serves 6

150 g (1 ½ cups) unsalted peanuts
1 Tbs peanut oil
60 g (½ cup) onion - minced
1 clove garlic - minced
1 red chili - seeded & minced
1 Tbs fresh coriander - chopped
1 Tbs fresh ginger - grated
1 Tbs fresh lime juice
1 Tbs honey
½ tsp shrimp paste
1 tsp salt
250 ml (1 cup) coconut milk*

*see essential ingredients list

Place the unsalted peanuts into an electric food processor and process until chopped coarsely. Heat the oil in a small pan and cook the onions, garlic, and chili until onion is golden brown. Add the peanuts and the rest of the ingredients and bring to boil. Turn down the heat and simmer, stirring frequently for 5 minutes until the sauce has thickened. Serve at room temperature and store in a sealed jar in the refrigerator.

Photo: Gado Gado

33

Goat's Cheese Tartlets

Makes 30

1 batch of cheddar cracker dough*
1 egg
1 tsp scd french cream^
120 g (½ cup) scd goat's cheese^
70 g (½ cup) black olives - pitted, sliced
70 g (½ cup) sun dried tomatoes - sliced
1 Tbs fresh basil - chopped
2 Tbs shallots - finely chopped

***see page 40 for recipe**

Preheat oven to 150°C/300°F
Lightly oil two small 12-hole muffin tins

Make the cheddar cracker dough and refrigerate for 15 minutes. Take the dough out of the refrigerator and split into 30 tablespoon size balls. Refrigerate the dough which is not in immediate use. Dipping fingers into cold water press the dough into the greased holes of the muffins tins, spreading it evenly and about 3mm thick. Bake for 15 minutes on 150°C/300°F. Remove the muffin tins from the oven and turn oven down to 100°C/210°F. Cover your forefinger with a thick dish towel. Lightly press the puffed up dough in the muffin tins down into the holes and place back into the oven, baking on low for 60 minutes. Remove from oven. Take the tartlet casings out of the muffin tins and sit on two layers of kitchen towels removing any excess oil. Let cool completely.

Combine the egg and french cream and then add the goat's cheese, olives, sun dried tomatoes, basil, and spring onions and mix gently. Fill the cooled down tartlet casings with the mixture, place on a baking paper lined baking tray and bake on 150°C/300°F for 15 minutes. Let cool before serving.

Lamb Koftas

500 g (1 lb) lamb - minced
60 g (½ cup) onion - finely chopped
1 clove garlic - minced
1 tsp dried ground coriander
1 tsp dried ground cumin
¼ tsp ground cinnamon
½ tsp green chili - finely chopped
1 tsp tomato paste*
1 Tbs fresh mint - chopped
1 Tbs fresh coriander - chopped
oil for frying

*see page 152 for recipe

Combine the lamb with all the other ingredients and mix well using your hands. Form into small balls, using about a heaped teaspoon per ball. Heat oil in a frying pan and cook the koftas until browned all over. Layer a bowl with some crumpled up kitchen paper and place koftas into the bowl to remove any excess oil.

Serve hot or cold. They can also be frozen and reheated in the oven when needed.

Yogurt Raita

1 fresh tomato- peeled and chopped
1 lebanese cucumber (small)
- chopped
1 clove garlic - minced
1 Tbs fresh mint - chopped
125 g (½ cup) scd yogurt^

Combine all the ingredients in a small bowl and mix well. Serve chilled.

Lima Beans Blinis

Makes 30

180 g (1 cup) dried lima beans*
6 eggs
1 Tbs scd french cream^
2 cloves garlic - minced
1 Tbs fresh rosemary - chopped
1 tsp salt
½ tsp pepper

*use only when symptom free

Preheat oven to 180˚C/360˚F
Lightly oil a small 12-hole muffin tin

Soak beans overnight. Drain and rinse under cold water. Cook covered in boiling water for up to 2 hours, until quite soft. Drain and place into an electric food processor. In another bowl combine the eggs and french cream^, and whip until fluffy. Pour into a food processor along with the garlic, rosemary, salt, and pepper. Blend all ingredients together until smooth. Pour about ½ cm of the mixture into the twelve hole muffin tin and bake in the oven for about 10 minutes. The blinis only need to set firmly and they do not need to brown. Repeat until all of the blinis are made. Refrigerate in an airtight container. These will keep for a few days and are great with any other toppings.

Lima Bean Dip

Makes 1 ½ cups

180 g (1 cup) dried lima beans**
480 ml (2 cups) vegetable stock*
120 g (1 cup) onions - chopped
1 tsp lemon rind - grated
1 tsp dried ground cumin
1 tsp dried oregano
1 tsp ground pepper
3 cloves garlic - minced
2 Tbs fresh dill - chopped
3 Tbs olive oil
60 ml (¼ cup) scd french cream^
juice of 1 lemon
salt to taste
chopped red peppers for garnish

*see page 145 for recipe
**use only when symptom free

Soak beans overnight. Drain and rinse under cold water. In a medium sized saucepan add the beans and the vegetable stock and simmer for up to 2 hours until they are quite soft. Drain the liquid and place the beans into an electric food processor. Add the remaining ingredients and blend until smooth. Refrigerate in an airtight container. When serving, garnish with the chopped red peppers.

Mexican Bean Nachos

Serves 4

170 g (1 cup) dried kidney beans*
1 Tbs olive oil
60 g (½ cup) onions - finely chopped
1 tsp red chili - minced
3 cloves garlic - minced
1 tsp dried cumin
1 tsp dried oregano
¼ tsp ground cloves
120 ml (½ cup) tomato puree**
salt and pepper

*use only when symptom free
**see page 152 for recipe

Soak kidney beans overnight, drain, and rinse. Place into medium sized saucepan, cover with water and bring to boil. Turn down the heat and simmer for up to 2 hours until the beans are soft. Drain the water from the beans. Heat the olive oil in a large skillet and add the onion. Sauté until onions are soft and golden. Add the chili, garlic, cumin, oregano, and cloves and cook for 1 minute. Add the beans and tomato puree and simmer until the sauce starts to thicken. Add salt and pepper to taste.

Serve the bean mixture with our cheddar crackers, scd french cream, grated parmesan cheese and our coriander and tomato salsa. When making the crackers add a little paprika to the dough, which will add a nice color to the crackers when baked.

Cheddar Crackers

Makes about 50 crackers

200 g (2 cups) almond flour
200 g (2 cups) sharp cheddar
1 tsp baking soda
1 tsp dried thyme
¼ tsp cayenne pepper
6 Tbs cold water

Pre-heat oven to 150°C
Line two baking trays with baking paper

Mix almond flour, cheddar, baking soda, thyme, and cayenne pepper. Add the cold water and mix to form into a flat dough. Cover and place into the refrigerator for 30 minutes.

Take the dough from the refrigerator and take about 1 teaspoon of dough and roll each one into a ball and squeeze down with your fingers onto the prepared baking tray. Each cracker should be about 3 mm/⅛ inch thick and at least 2 cm/¾ inch away from the next cracker. Bake in oven for ½ hour or until edges start to brown. The crackers still need to look pale in the centre. Turn the oven down to 100°C/210°F. Take the trays out of the oven and let cool for 5 minutes. Turn each cracker over and put the trays back into the oven. Bake for another ½ hour, turn the oven off, and let the crackers sit in the oven until the oven has cooled down. Take the trays out of the oven and let cool completely. Crackers should be slightly browned, but still pale. It is important not to brown beyond a faint golden hue, as the crackers will not taste good.

Store crackers between kitchen paper in an airtight container.

^All SCD yogurt items to be as per our home-made recipes.   Photo: Mexican Bean Nachos

Mini Chicken Satays with Peanut Sauce

Serves 4

500 g (1 lb) chicken breast fillet - deboned
120 ml (½ cup) coconut milk*
1 Tbs fish sauce*
2 tsp red curry paste**
1 tsp ground turmeric
1 tsp honey
1 Tbs fresh coriander – minced
salt and pepper
toothpicks soaked in water

*see essential ingredients list
**see page 150 for recipe

Pound the chicken flat and cut it into thin strips (about 2 cm/¾ inch wide). Combine the coconut milk, fish sauce, curry paste, turmeric, honey, and coriander, and marinate the chicken strips for at least one hour, covered in the refrigerator. Season to taste. Then thread each strip onto a toothpick. Heat some oil in a frying pan and fry the chicken for around 7 minutes turning them halfway through. They should be lightly browned and cooked through. Serve hot or cold with the peanut sauce.

Peanut Sauce 2

Makes about 2 cups

250 ml (1 cup) coconut milk*
1 Tbs red curry paste**
125 g (½ cup) chunky peanut butter
120 ml (½ cup) chicken stock***
2 Tbs honey
2 Tbs fresh lime juice
1 tsp salt

*see essential ingredients list
**see page 150 for recipe
***see page 145 for recipe

Pour coconut milk into a small saucepan and bring to boil. Whisk in the curry paste until dissolved. Add the peanut butter, chicken stock, and honey. Reduce the heat and simmer until smooth, stirring constantly, about 5 minutes. Remove from heat and add lime juice and salt. Set aside to cool to room temperature. Refrigerate in an airtight container.

Mini Spinach and Cheese Timbales

Makes 20

50 g (2 oz) red peppers - chopped
50 g (2 oz) baby spinach - chopped
1 Tbs butter
35 g (¼ cup) onions - chopped
40 g (½ cup) cheddar - grated
35 g (⅓ cup) almond flour
¼ tsp ground nutmeg
1 pinch cayenne
3 eggs
120 ml (½ cup) scd french cream^

Preheat oven to 150°C/300°F
Lightly oil a small 12-hole muffin tin

Place the chopped red peppers into the bottom of each muffin mould. Heat butter in a skillet and sauté onions until tender. Add the spinach and cook stirring constantly for about 1 minute, or until the spinach has wilted. Remove from heat and in a bowl combine the cheddar, almond flour, nutmeg, cayenne, eggs and french cream^, and mix well. Pour into the muffin moulds. Place the muffin tin into a baking tray filled with hot water to about half way up the tin. Bake in the oven for 15 – 20 minutes, or until timbales feel spongy. Cool slightly, remove timbales, and serve at room temperature.

Photo: Mini Spinach and Cheese Timbales

Pumpkin and Macadamia Nut Soup

Serves 4

2 Tbs olive oil
120 g (1 cup) onions – chopped
100 g (¾ cup) macadamia nuts
- roughly chopped
2 tsp fresh ginger – grated
2 cloves garlic – minced
1 tsp fresh turmeric or
½ tsp ground turmeric
225 g (1 cup) Granny Smith apples
- peeled, cored and diced
1 kg (2 lb) butternut pumpkin
- peeled, diced
250 ml (1 cup) chicken stock*
scd yogurt^ and macadamia nuts
for serving

*see page 145 for recipe

Heat the oil in a large skillet. Add the onion, macadamia nuts, ginger and garlic, and sauté until lightly browned. Add the turmeric and stir. Add the apple and pumpkin. Stir for 2 – 3 minutes and then add the chicken stock. Cover and cook for 20 minutes or until pumpkin is quite soft. Pour all the ingredients into a food processor and blend until smooth and creamy. Serve with a large dollop of SCD yogurt^ and whole or halved macadamia nuts. Add a little hot water if the soup is too thick.

Sweet Snacks

Dried Fruit Salad

Makes about 2 cups

4 ripe bananas - peeled
4 Granny Smith apples
- peeled, cored
2 pears - peeled, cored
4 kiwi fruit - peeled
juice from ½ lemon
1 Tbs honey

Slice the fruit into 5 mm/¼ inch slices. Mix the lemon juice and honey and dip the bananas, pears and apples into the mixture. Remove and place into the food dehydrator with the sliced kiwi fruit overnight for at least 8 hours.

Store in an airtight container. The kids will love this for a snack or in their school lunches.

Candied Orange Peel

Makes 1 cup

3 oranges
300 g (1 cup) honey
120 ml (½ cup) water

Cut both ends of the orange off and then slice into the peel lengthwise. Peel off the skin and use oranges for juicing. Cut the peel into 5 mm/¼ inch thick slices. Place the peel into a small pot of water and bring to boil. Drain the water and repeat the boiling and draining process 3 times. In another pot, bring the honey and ½ cup of water to boil. Turn down the heat and simmer for 10 minutes. Add the peel and simmer for 40 minutes until the orange peel turns translucent. Remove from heat and drain off the liquid and refrigerate in an airtight container.

Nut Butter Bites

Makes 45 - 50

140 g (2 cups) desiccated coconut*
300 g (2 cups) dried apples
160 g (⅔ cup) nut butter**
1 ½ tsp vanilla essence*

Combine all ingredients in a food processor and process until smooth. Take 1 teaspoon full of the mixture and form into a ball. Place into the food dehydrator and dry for 10 hours. Store the nut butter bites in an airtight container.

*check essential ingredients list
**use cashew butter, peanut butter or macadamia butter. Any nut butter is fine, as long as it does not contain any additives like sugar.

Photo: Dried Fruit Salad

Fruit Roll-Ups

Makes about 8

250 g (1 cup) apple & pear sauce*
250 g (1 cup) strawberries - hulled

*see page 156 for recipe

Combine the fruit in a food processor and process until smooth. Pour onto the flat dish of the food dehydrator and dry for 6 - 8 hours.

Store the roll-ups separated by waxed paper in an airtight container.

Kids simply LOVE these! Experiment by pureeing any kind of fruit and drying it.

Coconut Date Balls

Makes 30 - 35

150 g (1 cup) pitted dates**
150 g (1 cup) dried apricots*
150 g (1 cup) raisins
100 g (1 cup) walnuts
70 g (1cup) shredded coconut*
3 Tbs fresh orange juice
70 g (1 cup) shredded coconut
for coating

*see essential ingredients list
**see essential ingredients list under dried fruit

Cut all pitted dates in half, making sure all seeds have been removed. Combine dates, apricots, raisins, orange juice and walnuts in a food processor and grind to a paste. Add coconut and process again until the mixture is smooth. Place some cold water in a bowl and dip your fingers in the bowl. With moist hands, form small balls out of the date paste and roll in the shredded coconut.

Refrigerate in an airtight container.

The coconut date balls should only be eaten when already well advanced with the diet and you have been symptom free for at lest 3 months.

Pecan Caramel Toffees

Makes about 40

300 g (1 cup) honey
240 g (1 cup) nut butter*
2 Tbs butter
80 g (¾ cup) pecans - chopped

Place the honey into a medium sized pot and bring to boil. The honey will froth up. Keep boiling for about 8 minutes. Turn off the heat, add the nut butter, butter, and chopped pecans. Remove the pot from the heat and let cool for about 10 minutes. Place about 1 tsp of the toffee into individual candy cups and refrigerate. Eat at room temperature.

*use cashew butter, peanut butter or macadamia butter. Any nut butter is fine, as long as it does not contain any additives like sugar.

Spiced Honey-Glazed Nuts

Serves 6-8

500 g (4 cups) mixed nuts*
75 g (¼ cup) honey
1 tsp ground cinnamon
1 pinch ground cloves
¼ tsp turmeric
¼ tsp ground coriander
¼ tsp ground cumin

Preheat oven to 180°C/360°F

Spread the mixed nuts on a large baking tray and bake for 5-10 minutes, or until they are crisp and lightly browned. Remove and allow to cool. Keep a careful watch so they do not brown too much.

Combine the honey and all the spices and mix well.

Heat a large non-stick frying pan over medium heat and add the nuts. Sprinkle the spice mixture over the nuts and stir for 5 minutes or until nuts start to turn golden. The honey will heat and become thinner and coat the nuts. With a wooden spoon, gently separate the nuts if they start to stick together. When the nuts are cooked, remove them from the heat and spread them on a lightly oiled baking tray to cool.

Store the nuts in an airtight container.

*Do not use mixed nuts in a packet as most are coated with a starch coating. Make a mixture of SCD legal organic nuts such as almonds, brazil nuts, walnuts, cashews and pecans.

Photo: Pecan Caramel Toffees

Sides

Asparagus with Hazelnut Butter

Serves 4

24 asparagus spears - ends broken off
3 Tbs butter
3 tsp hazelnut meal
2 tsp cider vinegar

Bring water to boil in a vegetable steamer. Steam asparagus spears for 3 minutes, then remove. Melt the butter in a small skillet. Add the hazelnut meal and cider vinegar. Sauté for 3 minutes. Pour over the asparagus spears when serving.

Beans with Parsley Sauce

Serves 4

200 g (6 oz) green beans - tips cut and sliced in half lengthwise
1 Tbs butter
2 shallots - chopped
30 g (1 cup) fresh parsley - minced
2 tsp fresh dill - chopped
120 g (½ cup) scd french cream^

Steam the beans for about 5 minutes then set aside. In a medium skillet melt the butter and add the shallots. Stir and sauté until they have softened. Add the parsley and dill and cook for 2 minutes. Turn down the heat to low and add the french cream^. Add the beans and stir until the beans are well covered with the sauce. Serve immediately.

Carrot and Zucchini Fritters

Serves 4

200 g (1 ½ cups) carrots - grated
200 g (1 ½ cups) zucchini - grated
4 shallots - finely chopped
2 eggs
80 g (⅓ cup) scd dripped yogurt^
¼ tsp cayenne pepper
salt and crushed black pepper
oil for frying

Combine all the ingredients in a large bowl and mix until well combined. Heat the oil in a large frying pan. Place about ¼ cup of the mixture for each fritter onto the frying pan. With a spatula, press the mixture into a flat fritter and fry on medium for about 5 minutes on each side.

Serve as a side dish to fish or meat, or enjoy them as a snack with our sweet chili sauce.

Carrots Almondine

Serves 4

500 g (4 ½ cups) carrots - peeled, sliced
40 g (¼ cup) raisins
60 g (¼ cup) butter
2 Tbs honey
2 tsp fresh lemon juice
¼ tsp ground ginger
20 g (¼ cup) sliced almonds - toasted

Preheat oven to 190°C/375°F

Cook carrots for about 8 minutes covered in a little water in a medium size pot. Drain and place into a 20 cm/8 inch square baking dish. Add the raisins, butter, honey, lemon juice, and ginger and bake for 35 minutes, stirring occasionally. Toast the almonds in a dry frying pan until lightly browned, and sprinkle on top of the carrots before serving.

Cauliflower Cheese

Serves 4

500 g (1 lb) cauliflower - cut into florets
50 g (2 oz) scd dripped yogurt^
1 Tbs scd yogurt^
1 tsp honey
30 g parmesan - grated
¼ tsp crushed black pepper
paprika

Preheat oven to 170°C/340°F

Steam the cauliflower for about 5 minutes until slightly softened. Place into a medium size baking dish. Combine the dripped yogurt^ with the yogurt^, honey, pepper and parmesan and mix until smooth. Pour over the top of the cauliflower. Sprinkle with paprika and bake in the oven for about 10-15 minutes or until the top starts to brown. Remove from oven and let stand for about 10 minutes before serving.

Creamed Carrots

Serves 4

250 g (2 cups) carrots - peeled and chopped
1 Tbs butter
1 tsp honey
1 Tbs scd french cream^
salt and crushed black pepper

Boil carrots for about 5 minutes until soft. Drain and add the carrots with the rest of the ingredients in a food processor and blend until smooth. Season to taste.

Serve immediately.

Fragrant Cauliflower Rice

Serves 4 - 5

1 Tbs olive oil
½ tsp ground cumin
½ tsp ground coriander
½ tsp fresh ginger – grated
600 g (4 cups) cauliflower
- cut into small florets
80 ml (⅓ cup) water

Heat the oil on medium in a frying pan. Add the cumin, coriander, and ginger, and stir until fragrant. Add the cauliflower to the pan and stir until the spices cover the cauliflower. Add the water and cover with a lid and cook for 10 minutes on medium to low until the cauliflower is just tender.

Lima Bean Mash

Serves 4

180 g (1 cup) dried lima beans*
1 clove garlic – minced
½ tsp salt
½ tsp pepper
1 Tbs olive oil
½ lemon – juice and rind grated

*use only when symptom free

Soak the lima beans overnight. Discard water and rinse. Transfer the beans into a medium size saucepan and cover with water. Bring to boil and simmer for up to 2 hours until the beans have softened. Drain and place the beans in a food processor, adding the garlic, salt, pepper, olive oil and the juice from a half lemon. Process until smooth. Serve with the grated lemon rind sprinkled on top.

Minted Mashed Peas

Serves 4

1 Tbs olive oil
3 shallots - trimmed and chopped
250 ml (1 cup) chicken stock*
450 g (3 cups) frozen baby peas
1 tsp honey
¼ cup fresh mint - chopped
75 g (⅓ cup) parmesan cheese - grated
salt and pepper

* see page 145 for recipe

Heat the olive oil in a medium size frying pan. Add the shallots and sauté until tender. Set aside. Heat chicken stock in a small pot until boiling. Add the peas, honey, and mint. Cover and cook for about 4 - 5 minutes until peas are tender. Drain and reserve about 80ml/⅓ cup of the liquid. Return pea mixture to pan, adding the reserved liquid, and combine with the fried shallots. Roughly mash using a potato masher. Stir in the parmesan and season with salt and pepper.

Pumpkin and Cauliflower Mash

Serves 4

500 g (3 ⅓ cup) fresh pumpkin - peeled, diced
200 g (1 cup) cauliflower -
cut into large florets
35 g (3 ½ Tbs) butter
30 g (¼ cup) cheddar - grated
salt and pepper to taste

Cover pumpkin with cold water in a medium size saucepan, bring to boil and simmer for 5 minutes. Add the cauliflower and simmer for another 5 minutes or until both vegetables are soft. Place into a food processor with the remaining ingredients and blend until smooth.

Pumpkin Chips

Serves 6

100 g (1 cup) fresh pumpkin - sliced
grapeseed oil or sunflower oil

Place enough oil into a small skillet to cover the pumpkin. Heat the oil until a wooden spoon inserted produces bubbles. Then place the pumpkin slices into the heated until they turn brown, about 15-20 seconds. Remove with a slotted spoon and place onto 2 layers of kitchen paper, removing excess oil.

Sauteed Lima Beans

Serves 4

200 g (1 cup) lima beans*
2 Tbs olive oil
2 cloves garlic - minced
2 Tbs fresh lemon juice
salt and pepper

***use only when symptom free**

Soak lima beans overnight. Drain, rinse and cook in fresh water and 1 Tbs of olive oil for up to 2 hours or until soft. Drain the lima beans and combine with the rest of the olive oil and garlic in a medium size frying pan. Sauté on medium heat for 2 - 3 minutes. Then add the lemon juice, salt and pepper to taste. Cook for another minute, and then serve.

Sauteed Mushrooms

Serves 4

50 g (2 oz) butter
4 cloves garlic - minced
250 g (2 ½ cups) mushrooms
- whole or halved
salt and pepper to taste
60 ml (¼ cup) dry red wine*

*** see essential ingredients list**

Melt the butter in a saucepan over medium heat and add the garlic, stirring for 1 minute. Add the mushrooms, salt, and pepper, and sauté for about 5 minutes. Add the red wine and cook a couple of minutes longer. Serve immediately.

Steamed Asian Greens

Serves 4

4 baby bok choy
1 Tbs sesame oil
1 tsp red wine vinegar
1 Tbs honey
¼ tsp cayenne pepper

Cut the ends off the bok choy, chop the stems, and shred the leaves. Steam the bok choy for 1 minute in the vegetable steamer. Heat the sesame oil on high in a medium skillet and add the bok choy, stirring constantly. Add the red wine vinegar, honey, and cayenne, stirring to combine for 1 minute. Remove and serve immediately.

Zucchini Pasta

Serves 4

4 large zucchinis

There are two ways of making this pasta. The first and easiest way is to purchase the Garnish Magic*. Peel the zucchinis and using the widest blade, rotate the zucchinis through the machine. A wonderful endless stream of spaghetti-like thread is produced. Dip the zucchini spaghetti into a pot of boiling water for no more than 20 seconds. Rinse under cold water and serve with a hot pasta sauce.

The other way is to peel the zucchinis and slice them into matchstick slices. This will take a lot longer but will taste just as good. Dip these zucchini sticks into boiling water for 30 seconds. Rinse with cold water and serve with a hot pasta sauce.

* Garnish Magic.
see www.ccccibs.com

Zucchini Shoestring Fries

Serves 6

3 medium zucchinis
100 g (1 cup) almond flour
1 egg
¼ tsp salt
¼ tsp ground black pepper
grapeseed oil or sunflower oil

Peel the zucchinis, slicing them into 5mm/¼ inch slices and then cut the slices into shoestring size slivers. Whisk the egg with the salt and pepper. Dip the zucchini fries into the egg and then into the almond flour. Pour enough grapeseed oil or sunflower oil into a small skillet to cover the zucchini fries. Dip the handle of a wooden spoon into the oil and when it bubbles, the oil is hot enough. Place the crumbed zucchinis into the oil and deep-fry until they start to brown, about 15-20 seconds. Remove with a slotted spoon and place onto 2 layers of kitchen paper, removing excess oil.

Salads

Antipasto Platter

Serves 6

1 medium eggplant
1 medium zucchini
1 medium red peppers
10 cloves garlic
250 g (8 oz) button mushrooms
60 ml (¼ cup) olive oil
Salt and crushed black pepper

Preheat oven to 170°C/340°F
Oil the bottom of a large baking tray

Cut the ends off the eggplant and slice into 1 cm/½ inch thick slices. Place into a bowl and cover with cold salted water for 20 minutes. Meanwhile, seed the red peppers and cut into 2 cm/¾ inch wide strips. Place into a baking dish and grill under high heat until the skin starts to blacken. Remove from the grill and dip the red peppers into cold water. Then remove the peel and set aside. Drain the eggplant and place onto the baking tray. Cut the ends off the zucchini and slice into ½ cm/¼ inch thick diagonal slices. Peel the garlic and add to the baking tray. Slice the mushrooms, keeping the stems attached into halves and add to the baking tray. With a pastry brush, brush on the olive oil and sparingly season with salt and pepper. Place the tray into the oven and bake for about 1 ½ hours or until the vegetables start to brown slightly. Remove from oven and cool. Serve at room temperature or cold from the fridge.

Photo: Antipasto Platter

Apple and Duck Salad

Serves 4

4 duck breasts - deboned
1 Tbs honey
olive oil

110 g (½ cup) apple - peeled, chopped
110 g (½ cup) celery - chopped
80 g (1 cup) walnuts - chopped
8 cherry tomatoes - halved
100 g (3 oz) salad greens

Dressing

1 Tbs fresh basil
1 Tbs fresh parsley
6 sun-dried tomatoes
120 ml (½ cup) olive oil
juice from ½ lemon
1 tsp honey
salt and pepper

Set the oven to 210°C/410°F.

Brush the duck breasts with the honey and olive oil and bake in a covered casserole dish in the oven for 30 minutes or until they are cooked through. Remove from oven and let cool.

Meanwhile, combine the apple, celery, walnuts, tomatoes, and salad greens and toss well.

To make the dressing, combine the basil, parsley, sun-dried tomatoes, olive oil, lemon juice and honey in a food processor, and season to taste. Blend until smooth.

Shred the duck breast and layer on top of the salad. Pour dressing over and serve.

Chef's Salad

Serves 4

350 g (11 oz) chicken breast - deboned
1 cos lettuce
3 fresh plum tomatoes - quartered
100 g (3 oz) havarti - diced
1 lebanese cucumber - peeled, diced
3 eggs - hard boiled, peeled

Dressing

120 ml (½ cup) olive oil
60 ml (¼ cup) white wine vinegar
¼ tsp dry mustard powder*
1 Tbs dijonnaise**
1 tsp honey
¼ tsp pepper

*check healthfood stores for additive free mustard powder
**see page 146 for recipe

Steam the chicken covered in a small saucepan with a little water, salt and pepper for about 15 minutes or until cooked through. Let cool and slice into 1cm/½ inch slices.

Shred the cos lettuce and place into the bottom of a large bowl. Layer the tomatoes, havarti, cucumber, and chicken on top. Quarter the eggs and place on top. Mix all the ingredients for the dressing in a small screw top jar and shake until the dressing has thickened. Pour over the top of the salad shortly before serving.

BBQ Pear and Prosciutto Salad

Serves 4

6 slices prosciutto*
1 pear – peeled, sliced into 8 wedges
2 fresh plum tomatoes
– sliced into 8 wedges
80 g (⅓ cup) scd goat's cheese^
60 g (½ cup) red onion – sliced
200 g (6 oz) salad greens

Dressing
80 ml (⅓ cup) olive oil
1 Tbs white wine vinegar
¼ tsp dry mustard powder**
1 Tbs dijonnaise***
salt and pepper

*ensure it is sugar free
**check healthfood stores for additive free mustard powder
***see page 146 for recipe

Place the prosciutto in a large skillet and fry until crisp. Remove from the skillet. In a clean skillet, fry the pear and tomatoes with a little olive oil until slightly charred. Remove and let cool. Place the salad greens into a large bowl and top with the pear, tomato, onion, and crumple the goat's cheese^ over the top. Garnish with the prosciutto. Whisk together the ingredients for the dressing and drizzle over the top.

Black Bean Salad

Serves 4

200 g (2 cups) dried black beans*
1 ½ Tbs fresh coriander – chopped
1 Tbs fresh parsley – chopped
1 Tbs fresh lime juice
¼ tsp salt
¼ tsp ground black pepper
100 g (½ cup) tomatoes – chopped
120 g (½ cup) avocado – peeled, diced
2 Tbs shallots – chopped
1 Tbs green chili – seeded, minced
100 g (4 cups) salad greens

*use only when symptom free

Soak the beans overnight. Drain, rinse and place into a medium size pot. Cover with water and cook for up to 2 hours until the beans have softened.

Combine the coriander, parsley, lime juice, salt and pepper in a bowl and whisk. Add beans, tomato, avocado, shallots and chili, and toss well. Cover and chill for 2 hours. Combine with the salad greens shortly before serving.

Carrot and Raisin Salad

Serves 4 - 6

350 g (2 ¾ cups) carrots - peeled
and grated
80 g (½ cup) raisins
2 shallots – finely chopped
salt and pepper to taste
1 tsp fresh ginger – grated
2 Tbs fresh orange juice
1 clove garlic - minced
80 ml (⅓ cup) olive oil
1 tsp honey
1 Tbs red wine vinegar

Combine grated carrots, raisins, and shallots in a bowl and mix well. In another bowl combine salt and pepper, ginger, orange juice, garlic, olive oil, honey and red wine vinegar and whisk thoroughly. Pour over the carrots and serve chilled.

Chargrilled Zucchini and Herb Salad

Serves 4

450 g (14 oz) (3 medium) green
zucchini
450 g (14 oz) (3 medium) yellow
zucchini
80 ml (⅓ cup) olive oil
salt and pepper
1 tsp red wine vinegar
1 tsp cumin
2 tsp honey
1 Tbs pine nuts
1 Tbs fresh mint - chopped
1 Tbs fresh dill - chopped
25 g (1 oz) parmesan cheese - shaved

Cut the zucchini diagonally into thick slices and place into a large bowl. Add one tablespoon of oil and the salt and pepper and toss until the zucchini is evenly coated. Heat a grill pan until hot and fry the zucchinis until slightly charred and soft, about 2 - 3 minutes each side. Return to the bowl. Whisk remaining oil, vinegar, cumin, honey and add a little more salt and pepper. Pour dressing over the zucchini and leave to cool. In a dry pan, roast the pine nuts and before serving the salad sprinkle with the pine nuts and parmesan.

Photo: Chargrilled Zucchini and Herb Salad

Cantaloupe and Rocket Salad

Serves 4

½ cantaloupe - peeled, sliced
100 g (3 oz) rocket
2 avocados - peeled, sliced
½ red peppers - seeded, chopped
120 g (½ cup) scd goat's cheese
16 black olives

Dressing

60 ml (¼ cup) olive oil
2 Tbs white wine vinegar
¼ tsp dry mustard powder*
1 tsp dijonnaise**

*check healthfood stores for additive free mustard powder
**see page 146 for recipe

Place the cantaloupe on a large flat plate, layer the rocket, and avocado on top. Sprinkle the red peppers, goat's cheese, and olives over the top. Combine all ingredients for the dressing, whisking until well combined and pour over the salad.

Salad Nicoise

Serves 4

425 g (13 oz) tuna fillets
200 g (6 oz) green beans - ends chopped off
1 red onion - thinly sliced
4 fresh plum tomatoes - quartered
3 celery sticks - thinly sliced
3 eggs - hard boiled, quartered
12 anchovies
100 g (3 oz) nicoise olives
2 Tbs baby capers
2 Tbs fresh basil - shredded

Dressing

120 ml (½ cup) olive oil
60 ml (¼ cup) fresh lemon juice
1 clove garlic - minced
1 tsp honey

Sauté the tuna in a small skillet with a little water for about 10 minutes until just cooked through. Remove from heat and let cool. Steam the green beans until just soft, about 5 minutes. Slice the tuna into thin slices. In a large flat bowl, layer the onion, tomatoes, celery, and green beans on top of each other. Top off with the tuna, eggs, anchovies, olives, capers, and shredded basil.

Combine all the dressing ingredients in a screw top jar and shake until well combined. Then pour the dressing over the top of the salad shortly before serving.

^All SCD yogurt items to be as per our home-made recipes.   Photo: Cantaloupe and Rocket Salad

Chicken and Pineapple Coleslaw

Serves 4

500 g (1 lb) chicken breast fillet
130 g (1 cup) carrots - peeled, grated
350 g (3 ½ cups) savoy cabbage
- thinly sliced
250 g (1 cup) fresh pineapple - diced
2 shallots - chopped
20 g (¼ cup) fresh coriander - chopped
20 g (¼ cup) fresh mint - chopped

Dressing

250 ml (1 cup) coconut milk*
60 ml (¼ cup) fresh lime juice
2 Tbs fish sauce*
1 Tbs honey

* see essential ingredients list

Steam the chicken in a covered saucepan with a little water until cooked through, about 15 - 20 minutes. Let it cool, then shred. Combine with the carrots, cabbage, pineapple, shallots, and herbs. Whisk together all the ingredients for the dressing and pour over the top.

Green Salad

Serves 4

100 g (3 oz) Boston or Butter Lettuce
100g (3 oz) Spinach and Rocket

120 g (½ cup) scd yogurt^
60 g (½ cup) onion - finely chopped
2 tsp honey
60 ml (¼ cup) lemon juice
¼ tsp salt
pinch pepper

Wash the lettuce. Shred the leaves and place into a large bowl and toss with the spinach and rocket. Combine the onion, yogurt^, honey, salt, and pepper in a jar. Close the lid and shake until ingredients are well combined. Pour over the salad greens when serving.

Green Vegetable Salad

Serves 4

1 iceberg lettuce
150 g (5 oz) baby spinach
250 g (8 oz) cucumber - peeled, sliced
100 g (1 cup) celery - thinly sliced
100 g (1 cup) green peppers
- chopped
4 shallots - chopped
1 avocado - peeled, diced

Dressing

60 ml (¼ cup) olive oil
2 Tbs fresh lemon juice
½ tsp honey
¼ tsp salt
¼ tsp pepper
½ tsp dry mustard powder*
1 Tbs dijonnaise**
1 clove garlic - minced

*check healthfood stores for additive free mustard powder
**see page 146 for recipe

Shred the lettuce and place into a large bowl. Add all the other ingredients and toss until mixed well.

Combine all the ingredients for the dressing in a screw top jar and shake until well combined. Pour over the salad and serve.

Photo: Green Vegetable Salad

Moroccan Broccoli and Cauliflower Salad

Serves 4

270 g (1 ½ cups) broccoli florets
270 g (1 ½ cups) cauliflower florets
130 g (1 cup) carrots - diagonally sliced
¼ tsp salt
½ tsp ground ginger
½ tsp ground cumin
¼ tsp ground coriander
¼ tsp ground nutmeg
¼ tsp cayenne pepper
3 Tbs scd french cream^
2 tsp cider vinegar
1 tsp honey
2 Tbs shallots - chopped

Steam the vegetables in a vegetable steamer for about 2-3 minutes. Rinse under cold water and drain well. Combine the salt, ginger, cumin, coriander, nutmeg, and cayenne. Add to the french cream^ with the vinegar and honey, and mix well. Pour over the cooled vegetables and garnish with the shallots.

Warm Roast Vegetable Salad

Serves 4

300 g (2 cups) fresh pumpkin
- peeled, diced
150 g (1 cup) carrots - peeled, diced
150 g (5 oz) green beans - ends
chopped off
250 g (8 oz) zucchini - thick diagonally
slices
8 whole garlic cloves - peeled
3 Tbs olive oil
salt and crushed black pepper

Dressing

5 Tbs olive oil
1 Tbs white whine vinegar
1 clove garlic - minced
¼ tsp salt
¼ tsp pepper

Preheat the oven to 200°C/390°F
Oil the bottom of a baking tray

Cut all vegetable into big bite sized chunks. Place the pumpkin and carrots onto the baking tray and drizzle with some of the olive oil. Lightly season and bake for 10 minutes. Then turn the vegetables and add the rest of the vegetables. Crush the garlic cloves a little, but keeping them whole, add to vegetables. Drizzle the rest of the olive oil over the top. Bake for 15 minutes and turn the vegetables with a spatula. Cook for another 10-15 minutes or until the vegetables are cooked through and have started to brown nicely. Remove from oven and let cool.

Combine all the ingredients for the dressing and pour over the vegetables. Toss the vegetables gently in the dressing. Serve warm or cold.

Prawn and Mango Salad

Serves 4

750 g (1.5 lb) cooked prawns - shelled
2 mangoes - peeled, chopped
1 small red onion - peeled,
thinly sliced
2 celery stalks - thinly sliced
2 Tbs fresh mint - chopped

Dressing

120 ml (½ cup) olive oil
60 ml (¼ cup) lime juice
2 tsp fresh ginger - grated
1 tsp honey
Salt

Peel the prawns, leaving on the tails. Gently cut along the upper ridge of the back of prawn and remove the black vein. Place the prawns into a bowl and add the lime dressing. Toss gently and then add the mangoes, onion, celery, and mint.

Either serve at room temperature or refrigerate for up to 3 hours before serving.

Combine all dressing ingredients and whisk.

Photo: Prawn and Mango Salad

Pumpkin and Goat's Cheese Salad

Serves 4

300 g (10 oz) fresh pumpkin
- peeled, diced
100 g (3 oz) watercress
60 g (¼ cup) scd goat's cheese^
70 g (2 oz) black olives

Dressing

5 Tbs olive oil
1 Tbs red wine vinegar
1 tsp honey
pinch of pepper

Cut the pumpkin in 1 cm/½ inch cubes and steam for 5 minutes. The pumpkin needs to be slightly firm and not soft. Place the watercress onto a large flat plate and distribute the cooled pumpkin over the top. Then distribute the goat's cheese^ and the olives evenly over the top. Combine all the ingredients for the dressing in a bowl and whisk until frothy. Then pour over the salad and serve.

Red Salmon Caesar Salad

Serves 4

300 g (10 oz) salmon fillet
salt and pepper
200 g (6 oz) cos lettuce - washed,
roughly shredded
4 eggs - hard boiled

Dressing

5 anchovies
1 egg
¼ tsp dry mustard powder*
1 Tbs dijonnaise**
1 clove garlic
180 ml (¾ cup) olive oil
2 Tbs fresh lemon juice

*check healthfood stores for additive free mustard powder
**see page 146 for recipe

Rub the salmon with some salt and pepper and steam it covered in a small skillet with a little water (about 15 minutes), until just cooked through. Set aside and let cool. Place the cos lettuce into a bowl, quarter the egg, slice the salmon, and add to the lettuce.

To make the dressing, place the anchovies, egg, mustard powder, dijonnaise, and garlic into a food processor and blend until smooth. Add a little oil (about 2 Tbs) and blend again. Keep adding the oil slowly while still blending. Then add the lemon juice and keep blending until the dressing starts to thicken. Refrigerate in an airtight container.

Thai Chicken Salad

Serves 4

350 g (2) chicken breasts
200 g (2 cups) chinese cabbage
- finely shredded
150 g (1 ½ cups) rocket
100 g (1 cup) fresh basil - shredded
1 fresh red chili - minced

Marinade

1 Tbs salt
6 cloves garlic
2 Tsp fresh lemon juice
1 cup fresh coriander - chopped
1 tsp pepper

Salad Dressing

1 Tbs fish sauce*
1 Tbs lemon grass
1 kaffir lime leaf
1 clove garlic
1 Tbs honey
1 tsp fresh ginger - grated
2 Tbs fresh lime juice
50 g (½ cup) fresh coriander
1 tsp sweet chili sauce**
5 Tbs water

*see essential ingredients list
**see page 151 for recipe

Place all the ingredients for the marinade into a food processor and blend until minced. In a small bowl combine the chicken breasts and marinade. Let sit for 10-15 minutes. Place the chicken and marinade in a saucepan with ½ cup of water and simmer covered for 20 minutes or until chicken is cooked through. Let cool.

Combine all salad dressing ingredients in the food processor and process until all ingredients are finely minced. Take the cooled chicken and shred by hand. Combine in a large bowl with the shredded cabbage, rocket, basil and chili, and pour over the salad dressing, mixing well. Serve immediately.

Main Dishes

Beef Burgers with the Lot

Makes 6

500 g (1 lb) prime beef - minced
35 g (⅓ cup) onions - finely chopped
2 Tbs tomato paste*
2 eggs
1 tsp dry mustard powder**
¼ tsp ground cayenne pepper
50 g (½ cup) almond flour
havarti cheese – sliced

*see page 152 for recipe
**check healthfood stores for additive free mustard powder

Combine all ingredients except for the havarti cheese. Knead together with your hands, and shape into patties. Heat some oil in a large skillet and fry patties 5 minutes on each side until they are cooked through. Cut the onion rolls in half and grill for a few minutes on each side. Place the patty onto one-half of the burger and garnish with onion relish*, bbq sauce*, dijonnaise* and some slices of havarti cheese. Place the top of the burger back and enjoy!

Serve with pumpkin chips and zucchini shoestring fries.

*see condiments section for recipes

Crusty Onion Rolls

Makes 6

300 g (3 cups) almond flour
1 tsp baking soda
110 g (1 cup) cheddar - grated
1 tsp salt
1 tsp ground pepper
35 g (⅓ cup) onions - finely chopped
60 g (¼ cup) butter - softened
2 Tbs honey
2 eggs
olive oil

Preheat oven to 170°C/330°F
Line a baking tray with baking paper

Combine the almond flour with the baking soda, cheddar, salt, pepper, and onions. In another bowl, whisk the butter with the honey and eggs until frothy. Add the almond flour mixture to the egg mixture and knead together. With slightly moist hands, form the dough into 6 buns and place onto the lined baking tray. Trace a cross across the top of the rolls with a sharp knife and brush with oil. Place a heatproof dish with water into the bottom of the oven (this will make the rolls nice and crusty). Bake for about 15 minutes, then turn oven down to 150°C/300°F and bake for another 15 minutes. The rolls should feel firm and be nicely browned. Remove from oven and let cool. Refrigerate in an airtight container.

Photo: Beef Burger with the Lot, Crusty Onion Roll, Pumpkin Chips, and Zucchini Shoestring Fries

Beef Lasagna

Serves 4

1 Tbs olive oil
110 g (1 cup) onions - finely chopped
3 cloves garlic - minced
500 g (1 lb) prime beef - minced
130 g (1 cup) carrots - grated coarsely
1 tsp thyme - dried or fresh
1 tsp dried oregano
1 Tbs fresh basil - chopped
½ tsp salt
1 tsp ground black pepper
250 ml (1 cup) tomato puree*
300 g (1 ½ cups) fresh plum tomatoes,
- peeled, chopped
500 g (2 ½ cups) medium zucchinis
125 g (1 cup) cheddar cheese - grated
125 g (1 cup) parmesan cheese - grated

*see page 152 for recipe

Preheat oven to 180°C/350°F
Use a 23 x 33 cm /9 x 13 inch square Pyrex baking dish

Heat the olive oil in a large saucepan. Add the onion and garlic. Cook until tender. Add the minced beef and sauté until browned all over. Add the grated carrot, thyme, oregano, basil, salt, and pepper. Stir and pour in the tomato juice and chopped tomatoes. Simmer on medium heat about 30 minutes — until the sauce has become a very thick consistency.

Slice the zucchinis lengthwise into thin slices. Pour a small amount of sauce to cover the bottom of the Pyrex dish. Add a layer of zucchini slices, pour half of the sauce onto the zucchini layer, and top with half of the cheddar and parmesan. Add another layer of zucchini and top with meat sauce and cheese.

Bake in the oven for about 45 minutes or until the cheese starts to brown. Remove from oven and serve immediately. This dish freezes well and can be re-heated either in the oven or in the microwave.

Some moisture will be released from the meat and vegetables and accumulate in the bottom of the baking tray. The moisture will thicken up when the lasagna is stored in the fridge overnight. This dish is great reheated the next day.

Beef Stroganoff

Serves 4

500 g (1 lb) sirloin or tenderloin
6 Tbs butter
40 g (⅓ cup) onions - chopped
200 g (6 oz) mushrooms - sliced
pinch nutmeg
½ tsp dried tarragon
100 g (1 cup) scd french cream^
salt and crushed black pepper

Cut the meat into thin 2 ½ x 6 cm/1 x 2 ½ inch strips. Melt 3 Tbs of the butter in a large skillet on medium heat. Increase the heat and add the beef strips. Cook the beef quickly, browning about 1½ minutes on each side. Set the beef aside in a bowl. In the same skillet, reduce the heat to medium and add the shallots, cooking for about 2 minutes. Transfer the shallots to the same bowl as the meat and set aside. Add the other 3 Tbs of butter to the pan and increase the heat slightly, adding the mushrooms, nutmeg and tarragon. Stir and cook for about 4 minutes. Reduce the heat to low and add the french cream^ to the mushrooms. Stir and combine well. Add the meat, shallots, and season to taste. Stir and simmer on low for about 2 minutes.

Serve immediately with our cauliflower cheese.

^All SCD yogurt items to be as per our home-made recipes.

Photo: Beef Stroganoff

Chicken Burgers

Makes 8

50 g (½ cup) macadamia nuts
- roughly chopped
100 g (¾ cup) cashews
500 g (1 lb) chicken - minced
- roughly chopped
2 cloves garlic - minced
2 shallots - chopped
1 small handful coriander - chopped
grated lemon rind from 2 lemons
3 egg whites
salt and pepper

Place macadamia nuts and cashews into a food processor and process until roughly chopped. Combine with the rest of the ingredients and mix thoroughly by hand. Moisten hands and form the mixture into eight balls. Coat a large skillet with oil and press chicken burgers into patties. Fry them for 4 minutes on each side with the lid on the frying pan or until they are cooked through.

Serve hot or cold with our dijonnaise or sweet chili sauce.

Chicken Meatloaf

Serves 6

500 g (1 lb) chicken - minced
2 egg whites
1 shallot - finely sliced
65 g (½ cup) carrots - peeled, grated
65 g (½ cup) red peppers
- finely chopped
100 g (1 cup) fresh shiitake mushrooms
- finely chopped
1 tsp fresh ginger - grated
1 clove garlic - minced
20 g (¼ cup) fresh coriander - chopped
20 g (¼ cup) fresh chives - chopped

Preheat the oven to 175°C/350°F
Line a 10 x 21 cm/4 x 8 inch loaf pan with baking paper

Combine all the ingredients and mix well with your hands. Pack the ingredients into the prepared loaf tin and bake in the oven for 50 - 60 minutes, until the loaf is cooked through and golden on top. Remove from the oven and let stand for 10 minutes. Serve cut into slices with a salad or steamed greens.

Chicken Schnitzel

Serves 4

1 egg
½ tsp salt
¼ tsp black pepper
100 g (1 cup) almond flour
50 g (½ cup) parmesan cheese - grated
4 chicken thighs (or veal) - deboned and flattened
olive oil
1 lemon

Beat the egg with the salt and pepper in a bowl. Mix almond flour and parmesan in a separate bowl. Sprinkle a quarter of the almond mixture on the plate. Lift one flattened chicken thigh into the egg mixture and dunk thoroughly. Let the excess drip off and press both sides of the chicken into the almond mixture. Keep turning the chicken until well covered with the almond mixture. Set aside and continue with the other thigh fillets using the rest of the almond flour.

In a large non-stick pan, cover the bottom with olive oil and fry the chicken fillets on each side for about 4 minutes or until nicely browned. When done, take the cooked chicken out of the pan and place it on kitchen paper to remove excess oil before transferring to a plate.

Serve with a quarter lemon each.

Photo: Chicken Meatloaf

Chicken and Carrot Soup

Stock

Makes 2.5 Liters (10 cups)

**1 ½ kg (3 lb) chicken pieces
- with bones
10 small carrots - or baby carrots
3 stalks celery - chopped
1 bunch fresh parsley - chopped
80 g (1 cup) onion - peeled, chopped
3 cloves garlic
3 liters (12 cups) water**

Soup

Serves 4

**500 g (1 lb) chicken thighs - de-boned
6 small carrots - or baby carrots**

Place the chicken pieces in a large pot or slow cooker. Add peeled and roughly chopped carrots, celery, parsley, onion, and whole garlic cloves. Pour in the water and, if cooking in a large pot, bring to boil then lower the heat, skimming off any scum which forms on the surface. Simmer, covered on low for at least 4 hours. If you are using a slow cooker, set it on low with the lid, and cook 6-8 hours. Let the stock cool down, and then remove all the chicken and vegetables by straining through a sieve and discard.

To complete the soup, take 1.5 liters of the stock and freeze the rest for use in other dishes. Pour the stock into a pot. Dice the chicken, peel and dice the carrots, and add to the stock. Cook for about 30 minutes or until chicken is cooked through. Take out a third of the chicken and carrots and blend in a food processor until smooth. Add this back to the chicken soup. This will thicken the soup.

Chicken Vol Au Vents

Serves 4

450 g (13 oz) chicken thighs - deboned
½ tsp dried thyme
4 peppercorns
60 ml (¼ cup) water
1 Tbs butter
1 clove garlic - crushed
100 g (1 cup) mushrooms – chopped
125 g (4 oz) brie
60 g (2 oz) butter
80 g (⅓ cup) scd yogurt^
lettuce leaves for casings
parmesan cheese to taste

Cook the chicken, thyme, peppercorns, and water in a covered pot over medium heat for 30 minutes. Remove from heat and drain. With a fork and knife cut the chicken into small cubes. Melt the butter in a saucepan and sauté the mushrooms with garlic for 10 minutes until the mushrooms have softened. Set aside. Peel the skin off the chilled brie and cut into chunks. In a double broiler* place the brie and the butter, and heat until both have melted, using a whisk to stir frequently. When the two have combined, remove the dish from the heat and add the yogurt^. Place the cubed chicken into the saucepan with the mushrooms and bring back to heat. Add the brie sauce and stir until combined and warmed. Do not bring back to boil. Spoon the chicken mixture into the lettuce casings and serve with a sprinkle of parmesan.

*or place a heatproof bowl over a saucepan one quarter filled with water.

^All SCD yogurt items to be as per our home-made recipes.

Photo: Chicken Vol Au Vents

Dahl

Serves 4 - 6

250 g (8 oz) yellow lentils
2 Tbs ghee or butter
120 g (1 cup) onions - minced
2 cloves garlic – minced
1 tsp fresh ginger - grated
½ tsp ground turmeric
½ tsp ground cumin
¼ tsp ground cinnamon
¼ tsp mustard powder
1 sprig curry leaves
1 Tbs fresh coriander
3 fresh plum tomatoes - chopped
70 g (½ cup) green peppers – chopped
750 ml (3 cups) hot water
salt and pepper to taste

Soak the lentils overnight.

Drain the lentils and rinse with cold water. Heat the ghee in a large skillet and fry the onions, garlic, and ginger until golden brown. Add the herbs and spices and fry for a few more minutes until fragrant. Now add the lentils, tomatoes and green peppers and stir for 2 minutes until well combined. Add the hot water and bring to boil. Then turn down the heat and simmer, covered for 15-20 minutes or until lentils have absorbed the water and have reached a porridge like consistency. If there is too much liquid, leave the lid off and cook until it has reduced. Season and serve with pear chutney, scd yogurt and cauliflower rice.

Fish Fingers

Serves 4

**500 g (1 lb) deboned firm white fish
(flake or swordfish)
1 egg
Salt and pepper
100 g (1 cup) almond flour
Oil for frying**

Cut the fish into finger lengths. Beat the egg, salt and pepper in a small bowl. Place the almond flour onto a flat plate. Dip the fish into the egg and then into the almond flour, turning it to cover all sides.

Pour some oil into a non-stick frying pan and heat until hot. Place the crumbed fish fingers into the frying pan and fry on both sides until golden brown. Serve with a wedge of lemon.

Photo: Fish Fingers

Frittata Provencale

Serves 4 - 6

1 Tbs olive oil
1 clove garlic – minced
80 g (⅔ cup) onion – finely chopped
1 small bunch basil – destalked,
shredded
12 eggs
60 ml (¼ cup) scd french cream^
salt and pepper
100 g (1 cup) parmesan cheese – grated
70 g (½ cup) black olives – pitted
and sliced
70 g (½ cup) sun-dried tomatoes
– sliced
1 tsp dried oregano

Preheat oven to 180°C/360°F
Oil a 23 cm/9 inch round Pyrex pie dish

Heat the oil in a small pan. Sauté the garlic and onions until tender. Add the shredded basil leaves and sauté until wilted, about 30 seconds. Remove from heat and let cool. In the meantime whisk the eggs with the french cream^, salt and pepper until creamy. Add the parmesan and stir. Add the reserved cooked vegetables, olives, sun-dried tomatoes and oregano, and mix well. Pour the mixture into the pie dish and bake for 30 minutes, or until the frittata is firm to the touch. Let cool for 10 minutes before serving, or serve cold.

Frittata Verde

Serves 4

1 Tbs olive oil
60 g (½ cup) onions – finely chopped
1 clove garlic – minced
95 g (8) asparagus – chopped
75 g (½ cup) baby peas
125 g (4 oz) spinach – shredded
1 Tbs fresh coriander – chopped
1 Tbs fresh basil – chopped
125 g (1 cup) cheddar – grated
8 eggs
½ tsp pepper

Pre-heat oven to 180°C/360°F
Oil a 10 x 21 cm/4 x 8 inch loaf tin

Heat the oil in a pan and add onions. Sauté until tender, then add garlic, asparagus, and baby peas. Cook on medium for about 5 minutes, stirring frequently. Then add the spinach, coriander, and basil and stir until the spinach has wilted. Remove the pan from heat and let cool. In a large bowl, combine the cheese, eggs and pepper, and mix in the cooked vegetables. Pour the whole mixture into the prepared loaf tin and bake for 40 minutes, or until the centre of the frittata feels firm to the touch. Serve warm or cold.

Photo: Frittata Provencale

Lamb Cutlets

Serves 4

1 Tbs olive oil
1 tsp salt
12 lamb cutlets

Heat the olive oil in a frying pan until very hot. Sprinkle in the salt. Cook lamb cutlets for about 4 minutes on each side for medium and a little longer if you want them well done.

Minted Mashed Peas

Serves 4

1 Tbs olive oil
3 shallots – trimmed and chopped
250 ml (1 cup) chicken stock*
450 g (3 cups) frozen baby peas
1 tsp honey
¼ cup fresh mint – chopped
75 g (⅓ cup) parmesan cheese – grated
salt and pepper

*see page 145 for recipe

Heat the olive oil in a medium size frying pan. Add the shallots and sauté until tender. Set aside. Heat chicken stock in a small pot until boiling. Add the peas, honey, and mint. Cover and cook until peas are tender for about 4 – 5 minutes. Drain and reserve ⅓ cup of the liquid. Return pea mixture to pan, adding the reserved liquid, and combine with the fried shallots. Simmer for 1 minute, stirring frequently. Remove from heat and roughly mash using a potato masher. Stir in the parmesan and season with salt and pepper.

Mint Sauce

Makes 1 cup

110 g (1 ¼ cup) fresh mint
250 ml (1 cup) white vinegar
6 Tbs honey
3 Tbs fresh lemon grass – finely minced

Place 1 cup of the mint In a food processor, reserving the leftover ¼ cup mint for later. Add the vinegar and process until pureed. Scrape into a small saucepan and add the honey and lemon grass. Cook and stir over medium heat until the honey has dissolved. Reduce the heat to simmer, cover, and cook for about 20 minutes. Strain the sauce into a small serving bowl and let cool. Chop the remaining mint and mix into the strained sauce.

Photo: Lamb Cutlets, Minted Mashed Peas and Mint Sauce

Moroccan Chicken Tagine

Serves 4

Olive oil
240 g (2 cups) onions - chopped
1.5 kg (3 lb) chicken pieces
2 cinnamon sticks
½ tsp turmeric
1 tsp black pepper
500 ml (2 cups) chicken stock*
100 g (⅔ cup) dried apricots**
100 g (⅔ cup) dried prunes**
85 g (¼ cup) honey
1 tsp ground cinnamon
1 ½ Tbs almond flour
50 g (½ cup) slivered almonds

*see page 145 for recipe
*see essential ingredients list

Turn slow cooker to high. In a saucepan, heat a small amount of oil and sauté the onions until soft and then add into the slow cooker. Add the chicken with the cinnamon sticks, turmeric, and black pepper into the slow cooker and pour in chicken stock. Cover with the lid and cook for 2 ½ hours. Add the dried apricots, prunes, honey, cinnamon, and almond flour and stir until well combined. Cover with the lid and cook for another hour. In a dry pan, toast the slivered almonds. Serve the Tagine decorated with the toasted almonds.

This dish can be served with our lima bean mash, cauliflower rice or pumpkin and cauliflower mash. A little bit of scd yogurt^ on the side is delicious.

Layered Lamb Sandwich

Serves 6

500 g (1 lb) lamb - minced
120 g (1 cup) onions - minced
1 Tbs dried ground cumin
1 tsp ground allspice
100 g (1 cup) almonds - chopped
olive oil
salt and pepper

Filling
1 Tbs olive oil
80 g (⅔ cup) onions - minced
1 tsp ground cinnamon
1 Tbs dried ground cumin
500 g (1 lb) lamb - minced
80 g (½ cup) raisins
100 g (1 cup) pine nuts - toasted
salt and pepper

scd yogurt to serveˆ

Preheat oven to 180°C/360°F
Butter a 20 x 30 cm (8 x 12 inch) baking dish

Combine the lamb, onion, cumin, allspice, salt, pepper and almonds in a food processor and process until thoroughly mixed. Refrigerate until filling is ready.

To make the filling, heat the oil in a large frying pan over medium heat and cook the onions until golden and tender. Add the cinnamon and cumin and stir until combined. Add the lamb and cook stirring until the lamb is browned all over. Turn off the heat and mix in the raisins and nuts. Season with salt and pepper.

Retrieve the lamb mixture from the refrigerator. Spread half the mixture to cover the bottom of a 20 x 30 cm (8 x12 inch) baking dish. Spread the filling over the top. Take the rest of the lamb dough and place between two large sheets of baking paper. Roll the dough out until it is roughly the size of the baking dish. Remove the top layer of paper and invert the dough on top of the filling, peeling off the baking paper. Carefully mould the dough to cover the filling.

Brush with olive oil and bake for around 40 minutes or until the top is brown. Cool for 10 minutes before cutting. Serve with plain yogurtˆ.

ˆAll SCD yogurt items to be as per our home-made recipes.

Photo: Layered Lamb Sandwich

Osso Buco

Serves 6

1.5 kg (3 lb) veal shanks
1 tsp salt
1 tsp pepper
1 Tbs butter
60 ml (¼ cup) olive oil
120 g (1 cup) onions - minced
150 g (1 cup) carrots - minced
120 g (1 cup) celery - minced
3 cloves garlic - minced
1 Tbs fresh basil - chopped
1 Tbs fresh rosemary - chopped
1 tsp dried oregano
400 g (2 cups) tomatoes - peeled, chopped
250ml (1 cup) beef stock*
250 ml (1 cup) dry white wine**

*see page 145 for recipe
**see essential ingredients list

Have the butcher cut the veal shanks into 5 cm /2 inch thick slices. Rub the salt and pepper into the meat. Heat the butter and oil in a large skillet. Fry the veal on both sides until brown and crisp. Set aside.

In a food processor, mince the onions, carrots, celery, and garlic. Do not over process. Just blend until all vegetables are finely chopped. Transfer the vegetables into the heated skillet used previously and cook, stirring for 3 to 4 minutes. Remove from heat and place the vegetables into a slow cooker, adding the meat on top. Sprinkle the herbs over the meat and add the tomatoes, beef broth, and wine. Cover and cook on low heat for 8 to 12 hours. If using beef shanks instead of veal, cook the osso buco for at least 12 hours.

Serve with our lima bean mash or cauliflower rice.

Lamb Shanks in Red Wine

Serves 4

1.5 kg (3 lb) (6) lamb shanks
110 g (1 cup) red peppers - seeded, chopped
110 g (1 cup) celery stalks - chopped
4 cloves garlic - chopped
120 g (1 cup) onions - chopped
750 ml (1 bottle) dry red wine*
1 Tbs cumin seeds
1 ½ Tbs coriander seeds
2 Tbs olive oil
2 red chilies - seeded, finely chopped
400 g (1⅓ cup) tomatoes - peeled, chopped
3 Tbs honey
1 Tbs almond flour
130 g (1 cup) carrots - peeled, chopped

Place the lamb shanks into a large bowl with the chopped red peppers, celery, garlic and onion, and pour over the red wine. Leave to marinate in the refrigerator at least two hours or overnight. Drain the marinade from the lamb shanks and set aside.

Dry roast the cumin seed and the coriander seed in a small skillet. When they start to pop, remove from the heat and place into a mortar. Grind the seeds into a powder.

Heat the oil in a large skillet and fry the lamb shanks until they are browned all over. Place them into the slow cooker or a casserole dish. Add the reserved vegetable and marinade to the lamb. Then mix in the chilies tomatoes, honey, and almond flour. Scatter the reserved spices over the meat. If using a slow cooker, cook the meat on high for 3 hours and if using a casserole dish, cover and place into the oven at 180°C/350°F and cook for 2 hours, turning the shanks halfway through cooking and adding the chopped carrots. When done, drain the liquid from the meat, setting the meat aside, keeping it warm. Pour the liquid into a medium sized pot and bring to boil. Let bubble for about 10 minutes, reducing the sauce. Pour the sauce back over the meat and serve with our lima bean mash or pumpkin and cauliflower mash.

Photo: Lamb Shanks in Red Wine

Minestrone

Serves 8

250 g (2 cups) dried lima beans*
olive oil
240 g (2 cups) onions – chopped
2 cloves garlic – minced
2 pork ribs – de-boned, chopped
4 plum tomatoes – peeled, chopped
3 Tbs tomato paste**
3 Tbs fresh parsley - chopped
2 ¼ liters (9 cups) beef stock***
60 ml (¼ cup) dry red wine****
250 g (2 cups) carrots – peeled, chopped
80 g (⅔ cup) swede – peeled, chopped
225 g (2 cups) fresh pumpkin – chopped
160 g (1 cup) zucchini – chopped
110 g (½ cup) frozen baby peas
240 g (1 ½ cup) cauliflower – cut into florets
salt and pepper to taste
grated parmesan cheese to taste

*use only when symptom free
**see page 152 for recipe
***see page 145 for recipe
****see essential ingredients list

Soak lima beans overnight.

Drain, rinse and place into a large pot with water. Cook for 1 hour. Drain and place into a slow cooker. Heat oil in a medium size skillet. Sauté onions, garlic and pork ribs until the ribs are browned nicely. Place into the pot with the lima beans. Add the chopped tomatoes, tomato paste, parsley, beef stock and red wine, and cook covered for 2 hours on high for the slow cooker, or on medium heat for the large pot. After two hours, add the carrots, swedes and pumpkin, and cook for 30 minutes. Then add the zucchini, peas and cauliflower, and cook for another 30 minutes. Season and serve hot with a dollop of macadamia nut pesto and garnish with grated parmesan.

Mushroom and Spinach Roulade

Serves 4

2 Tbs butter
100 g (1 cup) mushrooms - chopped
120 g (1 cup) onions - finely chopped
200 g (6 oz) spinach - shredded
100 g (⅓ cup) scd dripped yogurt^
100 g (½ cup) scd french cream^
¼ tsp dry mustard powder*
1 Tbs dijonnaise**
pinch nutmeg
1 Tbs fresh tarragon - chopped
salt and pepper

*check healthfood stores for additive free mustard powder
**see page 146 for recipe

Heat the butter in a medium skillet and add the mushrooms and onions. Sauté until onions become soft. Add the spinach and stir until it starts to wilt. Add the dripped yogurt, french cream, mustard powder, dijonnaise, nutmeg, tarragon, salt and pepper, and stir on low heat until all is combined. Let the mixture cool. Meanwhile make the soufflé roll.

Place the soufflé roll onto a large piece of baking paper, then spread the mushroom and spinach mixture onto the soufflé roll and using the baking paper, roll the soufflé into a firm log. Wrap the baking paper around the roll and refrigerate to set (about 2 hours).

Soft Soufflé Roll

6 egg whites
4 egg yolks
pinch salt
100 g (⅓ cup) scd dripped yogurt^

Preheat oven to 150°C/300°F
Line a 9 x 13 inch (22 x 33 cm) glass Pyrex dish with baking paper

Whip the egg whites with the salt until stiff. Combine the egg yolks with the dripped yogurt^ until smooth and then gently fold under the egg whites. Pour into the prepared Pyrex dish and bake for 30 - 40 minutes until it starts to brown slightly. Remove from the oven. Place another piece of baking paper onto a flat cutting board and tip the Pyrex dish with the dough onto the cutting board. Remove the baking paper from the underside of the bread.

Photo: Mushroom and Spinach Roulade

Red Bean Burgers

Makes 10

200 g (1 cup) red kidney beans*
130 g (1 cup) sunflower seeds
55 g (½ cup) carrots - peeled, grated
60 g (½ cup) onion - finely chopped
60 g (½ cup) green peppers
- finely chopped
1 Tbs fresh parsley - finely chopped
1 Tbs fresh basil - finely chopped
salt and pepper
4 eggs
2 Tbs olive oil

*use only when symptom free

Soak the kidney beans overnight.

Drain and wash under cold water until the water runs clear. Place the beans into a pot and cover with water and cook for up to 2 hrs until soft, but not mushy. They should still have a slight firmness to them. Grind the sunflower seeds until the consistency of almond flour. Place the kidney beans into a food processor and process until coarsely chopped. Combine with the sunflower seed meal, carrots, onion, green peppers, herbs, salt, pepper and eggs, and knead with your hands until mixed through. Form into patties and fry in a skillet with the olive oil. Cook on medium for at least 10 minutes on each side. These burgers can be kept for up to 3 days and either eaten cold or reheated in the oven on 170°C/340°F for about 10 minutes. They will also freeze well.

Serve with our dijonnaise, sweet chili sauce or BBQ sauce.

Seafood Laksa

Serves 4 - 6

350 g (11 oz) deboned firm white fish
- (i.e. flake or swordfish)
1 red chili - finely chopped
2 tsp dried shrimp paste
160 g (2 cups) onions - chopped
1 tsp ginger - chopped
25 g (1 oz) macadamias
2 lemongrass spears (whites only)
- sliced thinly
2 Tbs peanut oil
1 tsp ground turmeric
1 Tbs ground coriander
1.5 ltr (6 cups) fish stock*
185 g (6 oz) crab meat
350 g (11 oz) prawns - shelled
400 ml light coconut milk***
4 shallots - sliced thinly
1 cucumber - sliced thinly
600 g (18 oz) (4 large) zucchini
- peeled, shredded**
1 small bunch vietnamese mint
- shredded

***see essential ingredients list

Place the white fish into a food processor and process until finely chopped. Form the meat into small balls (1 Tbs per ball) and set aside. Place the chili, shrimp paste, onions, ginger, macadamias, and lemon grass into the blender and blend into a paste. Use a little of the fish stock to help blend the mixture. Heat the peanut oil in a large skillet and fry the paste until it starts to brown. Add the turmeric and coriander, and fry for a few more minutes, stirring constantly. Combine the paste and fish stock in a large pot and bring to boil. Turn down the heat and simmer adding the crabmeat, prawns, and fish dumplings, simmering for about 15 minutes. Add the coconut milk and heat, but do not boil. Turn off the heat.

Pour the soup over the prepared zucchini vermicelli and top with the shallots, cucumber, and Vietnamese mint.

*Our local fishmonger sells frozen stock, which contains no sugars, or Soya or starches. Otherwise, purchase 500 g (1 lb) of whole green prawns and use the shells to make a quick stock by frying them in a little oil until they turn red. Then pour in 10 cups of water and cook until it is reduced to about 6 cups.

**To transform the zucchini into vermicelli, use the Garnish Magic* (see our purchase reference at the back of the book). Otherwise, peel the zucchini and slice into thin matchstick like slices. Place into a bowl and cover with boiling water for about 20 seconds. Then drain and rinse under cold water for a few seconds.

Spice Crusted Salmon

Makes 4 Servings

1 ½ Tbs whole dried coriander seeds*
1 Tbs dried cumin seeds*
1 Tbs sesame seeds*
¼ tsp dried thyme
1 tsp salt
½ tsp black pepper
4 salmon fillets with skin on one side
1 egg white
olive oil
*seeds are only for advanced diet and need to be crushed finely

Heat a dry skillet, toast the coriander seeds and cumin seeds, stirring constantly until they become fragrant. Remove seeds. Repeat the process with the sesame seeds. Remove from heat, add to the spices, and crush with a mortar and pestle. Add the thyme, salt and black pepper. Dip the skin side of the salmon fillets into the egg white. Then press into the spice mixture. Brush the skillet with olive oil and bring to a high heat. Place the fillets with the seeded side onto the oil. Fry on high for two minutes. Turn the heat to low. Flip the fillets and cook on low for up to 8 minutes, depending on how well done you would like them. Serve with our asparagus with hazelnut butter and sautéed asian greens.

Sri Lankan Curry Feast

Serves 4-5

3 Tbs ghee or oil
10 curry leaves
240 g (2 cups) onions – finely chopped
5 cloves garlic - minced
2 tsp ginger – grated
1 tsp ground turmeric
¼ tsp dried chili - ground
1 Tbs ground coriander
1 tsp ground cumin
½ tsp ground fennel
2 tsp ground paprika
2 tsp salt
2 Tbs vinegar
1.5 kg (3 lb) chicken thighs – deboned and cut into chunks
2 tomatoes – peeled and chopped
6 cardamom pods – bruised
1 stick cinnamon
1 stalk lemon grass - minced
250 ml (1 cup) coconut milk*

*see essential ingredients list

Heat the ghee or oil in a large frying pan or wok over medium heat. Fry the curry leaves until they turn brown. Add the onions, garlic, and ginger and cook until onions are golden and tender. Add turmeric, chili, coriander, cumin, fennel, paprika, salt and vinegar, and stir until well combined. Add chicken and stir until it is thoroughly coated with the spices. Add the tomatoes, cardamom, cinnamon, and lemon grass and cover. Cook over medium heat for 40-50 minutes. Uncover and add coconut milk and a squeeze of lemon if desired. Stir and cook uncovered for 2 minutes.

Serve with our cauliflower rice, orange & date chutney and cucumber raita.

Photo: Sri Lankan Curry Feast, Cauliflower Rice, Orange and Date Chutney and Cucumber Raita

Thai Fish Cakes

Makes 8

**400 g (13 oz) boneless white fish
- chopped**
1 tsp red chilies - chopped
2 tsp honey
2 tsp fish sauce*
4 kaffir lime leaves – chopped
80 g (½ cup) green beans – finely sliced
**100 g (½ cup) red peppers
- finely chopped**
olive oil

*see essential ingredients list

Place the fish, chilies, honey, fish sauce, and kaffir lime leaves into a food processor and process until smooth. Transfer the mixture to a bowl and add the beans and red bell pepper and mix thoroughly.

Heat a good amount of olive oil in a deep frying pan. Divide the mixture into 8 balls and shape into flat patties. Fry evenly on each side for about 4 minutes until golden and cooked through. Serve with our sweet chili sauce.

Thick Beef Sausages

Serves 4

8 thick beef sausages

Most commercial sausages have many additives, such as bread, coloring, sugar etc. Our local butcher is more than happy to make sausages for us. Our instruction to him is to only put pure beef or chicken mince, combined with egg and nothing else. We order two dozen from him at a time. Otherwise you will need to purchase a sausage maker (see our purchase reference guide) and make your own. The sausage world is your oyster once you get one of these machines. Check out our website for sausage making recipes.

Photo: Thick Beef Sausage, Pumpkin Mash, Sautéed Mushrooms and Sweet Onion Relish

Vegetarian Shepherd's Pie

Serves 4

110 g (1 cup) black beans*
150 g (1 cup) navy beans*
75 g (½ cup) green split peas*
75 g (½ cup) green lentils*
50 g (⅓ cup) carrots – peeled, chopped
50 g (⅓ cup) swede – peeled, chopped
50 g (⅓ cup) celery – chopped
120 g (1 cup) onion – chopped
120 g (1 cup) green peppers – chopped
60 g (¼ cup) butter
225 g (¾ cup) tomatoes – peeled, sliced
¼ tsp cayenne pepper
salt and pepper
120 g (½ cup) scd goat's cheese^
400 g (2 ½ cups) cauliflower – roughly chopped
25 g (1 oz) pecorino or parmesan cheese – grated

*use only when symptom free

Soak the black beans and navy beans separately overnight. Drain and rinse under cold water. Place the black beans into a pot with the split peas and the lentils and add about 725ml/3 cups of water and a little salt. Cover and simmer gently for up to 2 hours, or until the pulses have absorbed the water and are soft. Then remove them from the heat and mash them just a little with a fork. At the same time place the navy beans into another pot and cover with water. Cover and cook for the same amount of time as the black beans. Remove from the heat and drain.

Now preheat the oven to 190°C/375°F.

Steam the cauliflower until soft. Add the cauliflower and navy beans into a food processor and process until smooth, adding a little salt and pepper to taste. Set aside. Next, take the carrots, swede, celery, onion and green peppers, and process in the food processor until finely chopped. Melt the butter in a large skillet and add the vegetables. Cook them over medium heat for about 10 – 15 minutes. Set aside. Meanwhile, skin the tomatoes by dipping them in boiling for water for 1 minute. Remove with a fork, let cool a little and slide the skin off. Slice into thin slices.

Add the cooked vegetables to the pulses mixture and combine well. Season to taste. Pour the mixture into a 20 x 20 cm/8 inch square baking dish and arrange the tomatoes in overlapping slices on the top. Combine the mashed cauliflower and navy bean mixture with the goat's cheese^ and season with fresh cracked pepper. Spread the mixture over the rest of the ingredients in the baking dish. Finally top with the grated cheese and bake on the top shelf in the oven for about 30 minutes, or until the top is lightly browned. Let pie sit for 10 minutes after removing from oven, then serve. This will taste even better the next day.

Zucchini Bolognese

Serves 4

600 g (4 medium) zucchinis

50 g (2 oz) butter
180 g (6 oz) speck or bacon*
120 g (1 cup) onion - finely chopped
120 g (1 cup) carrot - finely chopped
1 celery stick - finely chopped
400 g (13 oz) lean beef - minced
150 g (5 oz) chicken livers - chopped
500 ml (2 cups) beef stock**
250 ml (1 cup) tomato puree***
125 ml (½ cup) dry red wine****
¼ tsp grated nutmeg
freshly grated parmesan cheese, for serving

To prepare the zucchini pasta it helps to have a Garnish Magic™ such as the one we use (see the reference guide). This garnish maker produces endless spaghetti like strands of zucchini. Otherwise cut zucchini into thin slices and then slice into thin strips.

Heat half the butter in a heavy-based saucepan. Add the speck or bacon and cook until golden. Add the onion, carrot, and celery and cook over low heat for 8 minutes, stirring occasionally. Increase the heat, add the remaining butter and mince. Break up any lumps with a wooden spoon and stir until brown. Add the chicken livers and fry until they change color. Add the beef stock, tomato puree, wine, nutmeg, and salt and pepper to taste.

Bring to boil, then simmer covered over low heat for at least 4 hours, adding a little more stock if the sauce becomes to dry.

Bring a large pot of water to boil, adding ½ teaspoon of salt. Dip the zucchini pasta into the boiling water for 15 seconds. Strain the zucchini and distribute into bowls, topping with the Bolognese sauce and parmesan to taste.

* Bacon has to be sulphur and sugar free. Otherwise eliminate it from the recipe.
**see page 145 for recipe
***see page 152 for recipe
****see essential ingredients list

Photo: Zucchini Bolognese

Pumpkin Gnocchi

Serves 4

1 kg (2 lb) fresh pumpkin
3 eggs
50 g (½ cup) parmesan cheese - grated
100 g (1 cup) almond flour

Preheat oven to 160°C/320°F
Line a 22 x 33 cm/9 x 13 inch baking dish with baking paper

Cut pumpkin into large chunks, leaving the skin on and remove seeds. Bake in the oven for 1 hour or until pumpkin is quite soft. Remove from the oven and let cool a little. Remove any hard skin and place the soft pumpkin into a food processor. Process until pumpkin is smooth. Add the eggs, parmesan and almond flour and process to combine. Pour the mixture into the prepared baking dish and bake in the oven for 1 hour or until the gnocchi feels firm. Remove from the oven and let sit for 5 minutes. Cut the gnocchi into diamond shapes and serve hot with our herb cream sauce.

Herb Cream Sauce

Serves 4

90 g (⅓ cup) butter
1 clove garlic - minced
1 Tbs basil - finely chopped
1 Tbs fresh tarragon - finely chopped
1 Tbs fresh parsley - finely chopped
4 sage leaves - finely chopped
250 ml (1 cup) scd french cream^
50 g (½ cup) parmesan cheese - grated
Salt and pepper to taste

Melt the butter in a small skillet on medium heat. Add the garlic and herbs and stir for 1 minute. Add the french cream^ and half the parmesan, reserving the rest for garnish. Stir and cook until the parmesan has melted. Season to taste. Do not boil the mixture, just sauté on low until all ingredients have combined to a creamy sauce.

Savory Condiments

BBQ Sauce

Makes 1.5 Liters (6 cups)

2 kg (4 lb) fresh plum tomatoes
400 g (2 cups) celery - chopped
200 g (1 cup) green peppers - chopped
120 g (1 ½ cups) onion - chopped
5 cloves garlic - minced
300 g (1 cup) honey
200 ml (¾ cup) vinegar
1 Tbs lemon juice
1 Tbs paprika
1 Tbs dried mustard
2 tsp salt
½ tsp dried chili - ground
½ tsp cayenne pepper

Chop tomatoes, place into a large pot and cook on medium heat about 20 minutes until soft. Press through a food strainer, removing all the skin and seeds. Place back into the pot and add all the other ingredients. Bring to boil, reduce heat and simmer, stirring often for 2 ½ hours or until thickened to your liking. Remove from the heat and let cool. Pour into food processor and process until smooth. Return to the heat and bring back to boil slowly, simmering and stirring frequently until the desired consistency, about 20 minutes.

Store in sterilized jars, or freeze for later use.

Caesar Dressing

5 anchovies
1 egg
¼ tsp dry mustard powder*
1 Tbs dijonnaise**
1 clove garlic
180 ml (¾ cup) olive oil
2 Tbs lemon juice

To make the dressing, place the anchovies, egg, mustard powder, dijonnaise and garlic into a blender and blend until smooth. Add a little oil (about 2 Tbs) and blend again. Keep adding the oil slowly while still blending. Then add the lemon juice and keep blending until the dressing starts to thicken. Refrigerate in an airtight container.

*check healthfood stores for additive free mustard powder
**see page 146 for recipe

Cucumber Raita

2 large cucumbers
2 tsp salt
1 clove garlic - minced
¼ tsp fresh ginger - grated
250 g (1 cup) scd yogurt^
fresh lemon juice to taste

Peel and slice cucumbers very thinly. Sprinkle with salt and refrigerate for about 1 hour. Place the cucumber in a strainer and pour off the liquid, squeezing out as much as possible. Mix the garlic and ginger with the yogurt^. Add the cucumber and stir, adding a squeeze of lemon juice to taste.

Chicken Stock

Makes 4 Liters (16 cups)

1 chicken carcass
500 g (1 lb) chicken thighs - with bones
130 g (1 cup) swedes - peeled, diced
120 g (1 cup) onions - peeled, diced
110 g (1 cup) celery - diced
150 g (1 cup) carrots - peeled, diced
3 cloves garlic - peeled, chopped
1 bay leaf
2 sprigs thyme
1 bunch parsley
4 ltr (16 cups) water

Place all ingredients into a large saucepan. Bring to boil, then cover and simmer on very low for 6 hours. Skim off any fat or scum which rises to the surface. Turn off the heat and let stand, cooling for 2 hours. Pour through a strainer, discarding the meat and vegetables. Freeze in 1 liter (4 cup) and ½ liter (2 cup) lots. The broth will last for up the 3 months in the freezer.

If using a slow cooker, place all the ingredients into the slow cooker and cook on low overnight.

Beef Stock

Makes 4 Liters (16 cups)

1.5 kg (3 lb) beef bones
60 g (½ cup) onions - peeled, diced
110 g (1 cup) celery - leaves, diced
150 g (1 cup) carrots - peeled, diced
3 cloves garlic - peeled, chopped
1 bay leaf
10 peppercorns
1 bunch fresh parsley
2 sprigs fresh thyme
4 ltr (16 cups) water

Place all ingredients into a large saucepan. Bring to boil, then cover and simmer on very low for 8 hours. Alternatively, place all ingredients into a slow cooker and cook covered overnight. Skim off any fat or scum which rises to the surface. Turn off the heat and let stand, cooling for 2 hours. Pour through a strainer, discarding the meat and vegetables. Freeze in 1 liter (4 cup) and ½-liter (2 cup) lots. The broth will last for up the 3 months in the freezer.

Vegetable Stock

Makes 4 Liters (16 cups)

120 g (1 cup) onions - peeled, diced
440 g (4 cup) celery - diced
450 g (3 cup) carrots - peeled, diced
3 cloves garlic - peeled, chopped
2 bay leaves
130 g (1 cup) swedes - peeled, diced
1 bunch fresh parsley
2 sprigs fresh thyme
4 ltr (16 cups) water

Place all ingredients into a large saucepan. Bring to boil, then cover and simmer on very low for 6 hours. Skim off any scum which rises to the surface. Turn off the heat and let stand, cooling for 2 hours. Pour through a strainer, discarding the vegetables. Freeze in 1 liter (4 cup) and ½ liter (2 cup) lots. The broth will last for up the 3 months in the freezer.

If using a slow cooker, place all the ingredients into the slow cooker and cook on low overnight.

Date and Orange Chutney

Makes 2 cups

2 oranges - peeled, seeded, chopped
270 g (1 ½ cups) dried dates - chopped**
3 Tbs vinegar
2 Tbs honey
½ lemon - juiced and grated rind
1 tsp mustard seeds*
1 Tbs ground cinnamon
pinch cayenne
60 ml (¼ cup) fresh orange juice

Combine all ingredients in a heavy saucepan and cook covered for 30-45 minutes, stirring occasionally. Add a little liquid if needed. Allow to cool before serving. Store in an airtight jar in the refrigerator.

*if seeds are not well tolerated replace with 1 tsp of mustard powder
**see essential ingredients list under dried fruit

Dijonnaise

Makes 1 cup

1 large egg
3 tsp dry mustard powder*
1 Tbs honey
1½ tsp vinegar
250 ml (1 cup) grapeseed oil
or sunflower oil
1½ Tbs lemon juice
½ tsp salt

Whisk the egg, mustard powder, honey, salt and pepper together. Add a very small amount of oil and whisk until combined. Keep adding small amounts of oil into the mixture and keep combining it. After about ¼ cup of oil, slowly pour the rest of the oil in a fine stream into the mixture while whisking. After half the oil has been used, pour in the vinegar and keep adding the oil while whisking.

The secret to good mayonnaise is to pour the oil into the mixture very slowly while whisking. Add salt, pepper and lemon juice to taste at the end. Stores for up to two weeks in the refrigerator in an airtight jar.

*check healthfood stores for additive free mustard powder

Green Chili Sambal

4 large green chilies - seeded
and finely sliced
2 shallots - finely sliced
1 small Granny Smith apple - peeled, cored
and finely chopped
3 Tbs fresh coriander - chopped
2 Tbs white wine vinegar
2 Tbs honey
3 Tbs fish sauce*
3 Tbs peanut oil

Combine all the ingredients in an food processor and process until finely chopped. Refrigerate in an airtight jar.

*see essential ingredients list

Guacamole

Makes 1 cup

2 avocados
2 Tbs fresh lemon juice
2 cloves garlic
½ tsp salt
½ tsp pepper

Scoop out avocado flesh into a food processor, add all the other ingredients and process until desired smoothness. Refrigerate in an airtight jar.

Hollandaise Sauce

Serves 4

3 egg yolks
2 Tbs water
175 g unsalted butter – cubed
2 Tbs fresh lemon juice
salt and pepper

Place a heatproof bowl over a saucepan filled a quarter of the way with water. Do not let the water boil, but keep it at a simmer. Place the egg yolks and water into the bowl and whisk for about 3 minutes until the mixture becomes quite thick and has doubled in volume. Add the butter, one cube at a time, ensuring the previous cube has melted completely. This will take about 10 minutes. Keep whisking until the sauce starts to thicken, then remove from heat. Whisk in the lemon juice and season with salt and pepper. An electric whisk will take the pressure off your arm and the preparation time will be reduced by about half. Serve immediately.

Herb Cream Sauce

Serves 4

90 g (⅓ cup) butter
1 clove garlic – minced
1 Tbs basil – finely chopped
1 Tbs fresh tarragon – finely chopped
1 Tbs fresh parsley – finely chopped
4 sage leaves – finely chopped
250 ml (1 cup) scd french cream
50 g (½ cup) parmesan cheese – grated
Salt and pepper to taste

Melt the butter in a small skillet on medium heat. Add the garlic and herbs and stir for 1 minute. Add the french cream and half the parmesan, reserving the rest for garnish. Stir and cook until the parmesan has melted. Season to taste. Do not boil the mixture, just sauté on low until all ingredients have combined into a creamy sauce.

Mint Sauce

Makes 1 cup

110 g (1 ¼ cup) fresh mint
250 ml (1 cup) white vinegar
6 Tbs honey
3 Tbs fresh lemon grass – finely minced

In a food processor place 1 cup of the mint, reserving the leftover ¼ cup mint for later. Add the vinegar and process until pureed. Scrape into a small saucepan and add the honey and lemon grass. Cook over medium heat and stir until the honey has dissolved. Reduce heat to a simmer, cover, and cook for about 20 minutes. Strain the sauce into a small serving bowl and let it cool. Chop the remaining mint and mix into the strained sauce.

Onion Relish

Makes 1 kg (4 cup)

1 kg (2 lb) sweet onions – chopped
60 g (½ cup) celery – chopped
100 g (½ cup) red peppers – chopped
1 Tbs butter – melted
180 ml (¾ cup) apple cider vinegar
60 ml (¼ cup) water
2 Tbs honey
1 tsp celery seeds*
¼ tsp salt

*if seeds are not well tolerated remove from recipe

Sauté onions, celery, and red peppers in butter in a medium pot for 15 minutes until the onions become translucent. Be careful not to brown the onions. Add the vinegar, water, honey, celery seed and salt, and simmer uncovered for about 20 minutes. Refrigerate in an airtight jar.

Parsley Sauce

Serves 4

1 Tbs butter
2 shallots – chopped
30 g (1 cup) fresh parsley – minced
2 tsp fresh dill - chopped
120 g (½ cup) scd french creamˆ
salt and pepper to taste

Melt the butter in a medium skillet and add the shallots. Stir and sauté until they have softened. Add the parsley and dill and cook for 2 minutes. Reduce heat to low and add the french creamˆ. Stir and remove heat. Season to taste and serve immediately.

Pear Chutney

Makes 1 ½ kg (5 cups)

1 ½ kg (5 cups) pears - peeled, cored and diced
300 g (1 cup) honey
500 ml (2 cups) cider vinegar
80 g (1 cup) onions - chopped
100 g (1 cup) raisins
20 g (¼ cup) fresh ginger - peeled, chopped
1 clove garlic - minced
½ tsp cayenne pepper
2 tsp salt
½ tsp ground cinnamon
½ tsp whole cloves
2 tsp mustard seeds*

*if seeds are not well tolerated replace with 1 tsp of mustard powder

Combine the honey and vinegar in a large pot and bring to boil. Stir to combine. Add the pears and remaining ingredients and mix well. Cook slowly on medium heat uncovered for about 1 hour, stirring occasionally. When the mixture has thickened remove from heat and pour into hot sterilized jars and seal.

Lime Dressing

120 ml (½ cup) olive oil
60 ml (¼ cup) lime juice
2 tsp fresh ginger - grated
1 tsp honey
Salt

Combine all ingredients and whisk.

Yogurt Dressing

120 g (½ cup) scd yogurt^
60 g (½ cup) onion - finely chopped
2 tsp honey
60 ml (¼ cup) lemon juice
¼ tsp salt
pinch pepper

Combine the onion, yogurt, honey, salt and pepper in a glass jar. Close the lid and shake until ingredients are well combined.

Peanut Sauce 1

Serves 6

150 g (1 cup) unsalted peanuts
1 Tbs peanut oil
60 g (½ cup) onion – minced
1 clove garlic – minced
1 red chili – seeded & minced
1 Tbs fresh coriander – chopped
1 Tbs fresh ginger - grated
1 Tbs fresh lime juice
1 Tbs honey
½ tsp shrimp paste
1 tsp salt
250 ml (1 cup) coconut milk*

*see essential ingredients list

Place the unsalted peanuts into a food processor and process until chopped coarsely. Heat the oil in a small pan and cook the onions, garlic, and chili until onion is golden brown. Add the peanuts and the rest of the ingredients and bring to boil. Turn down the heat and simmer, stirring frequently for 5 minutes until the sauce has thickened. Serve at room temperature. Store in a sealed jar in the refrigerator.

Peanut Sauce 2

Makes about 2 cups

250 ml (1 cup) coconut milk*
1 Tbs red curry paste**
125 g (½ cup) chunky peanut butter
120 ml (½ cup) chicken stock***
2 Tbs honey
2 Tbs fresh lime juice
1 tsp salt

*see essential ingredients list
**see next recipe
***see page 145 for recipe

Pour coconut milk into a small saucepan and bring to boil. Whisk in the curry paste until dissolved. Add the peanut butter, chicken stock, and honey. Reduce the heat and simmer until smooth, stirring constantly, about 5 minutes. Remove from heat and add lime juice and salt. Set aside to cool to room temperature. Refrigerate in an airtight jar.

Red Curry Paste

12 small dried chilies
4 Tbs fresh garlic - chopped
4 Tbs shallots - chopped
2 Tbs fresh lemon grass - minced
1 Tbs fresh coriander - chopped
½ tsp fresh lime rind
1 tsp shrimp paste
½ tsp salt
¼ crushed black pepper

Soak dried chilies in hot water for 15 minutes. Drain and place into a blender with the rest of the ingredients, except for the shrimp paste. Blend until well mixed and then add the shrimp paste and process until smooth.

Refrigerate in an airtight jar for up to 4 months.

Simple Salad Dressing

80 ml (⅓ cup) olive oil
1 Tbs white wine vinegar
¼ tsp dry mustard powder*
1 Tbs dijonnaise**
salt and pepper

*check healthfood stores for additive free mustard powder
**see page 146 for recipe

Place all the ingredients into a screw top jar and shake until well combined.

Sun-Dried Tomatoes

Makes 400 g (13 oz)

16 fresh plum tomatoes
80 ml (⅓ cup) olive oil
salt

Preheat the oven to 180°C
Oil the bottom of a baking tray

Cut the tomatoes in half and generously lather with the olive oil. Sprinkle sparingly with salt and cook in the oven for 2 hours, until the tomatoes have shriveled to one third their size. Remove from the oven and let cool completely. Refrigerate in an airtight container with a little olive oil.

Sweet Chili Sauce

Makes 1 liter (4 cup)

10 cloves garlic - minced
4 large red chilies - chopped
2 large red peppers - chopped
3 Tbs fresh ginger - grated
8 kaffir lime leaves - chopped
3 lemon grass stems - chopped
1 bunch coriander - chopped
300 g (1 cup) honey
4 Tbs water
100 ml (3 fl. oz) apple cider vinegar
50 ml fish sauce*
1 tsp salt

*see essential ingredients list

Combine garlic, chilies, red peppers, ginger, lime leaves, lemongrass, and coriander in a food processor and process until finely chopped. Combine honey and water in a medium size saucepan and heat until honey starts to simmer. Add the paste, apple cider vinegar, fish sauce and salt, and simmer for about 2 minutes. For a spicier sauce, try leaving in some of the chili seeds. Refrigerate in an airtight jar.

Tomato and Coriander Salsa

Makes 4 cups

900g (3 cups) tomatoes – chopped
60 g (½ cup) onions – finely chopped
1 – 2 green jalapeno peppers
– seeded, minced
1 small bunch coriander – chopped
1 tsp honey
3 Tbs fresh lime juice

Combine all ingredients in a large bowl and mix. Refrigerate in an airtight jar. The flavors will improve over 24 hours.

Tomato Paste

Makes 1 cup

2 kg (4 lb) fresh plum tomatoes
60 g (½ cup) celery – chopped
130 g (1 cup) carrots – chopped
120 g (1 cup) onions – chopped
2 Tbs fresh basil – chopped
½ tsp fresh rosemary
2 tsp salt
½ tsp cinnamon
6 whole cloves
8 peppercorns
2 cloves garlic – chopped

Core tomatoes, no need to peel them, and chop coarsely. Combine all ingredients in a large saucepan and bring to boil. Turn down the heat and simmer covered for about 30 minutes, stirring occasionally. Press the ingredients through a sieve, discarding the leftovers. Return the sauce to the saucepan and cook for 3 hours on very low heat, stirring occasionally. When the sauce has thickened sufficiently let cool and store in ice cube trays in the freezer.

Tomato Puree

Makes 4 x 500 ml (2 cup) jars

16 kg (32 lb) ripe plum tomatoes
2 Tbs Salt
360 g (3 cups) onion – chopped
olive oil

Sterilize the jars (check our website for how to do this)

Bring a large pot of water to the boil. Add the whole tomatoes into the hot water for about 1 minute. Drain and run under cold water. The peel will now easily slide off.

Core the tomatoes. Place the tomatoes into a food processor and process in batches until smooth. Place a little oil into the large pot and sauté the onions until they are soft and translucent. Add the tomato puree and salt, and simmer covered for about 45 minutes. Stir occasionally. When sufficiently thickened, remove from heat and store in the refrigerator in sterilized jars. Alternatively, freeze in batches.

Macadamia Nut Pesto

180 g (2 cups) sweet basil
60 g (¼ cup) parmesan cheese - grated
120 ml (½ cup) olive oil
3 cloves garlic
35 g (⅓ cup) macadamia nuts

Combine all ingredients in a food processor and process until smooth or slightly chunky. Refrigerate in an airtight jar.

Yogurt Raita

1 fresh tomato- peeled and chopped
1 lebanese cucumber -
chopped
1 clove garlic - minced
1 Tbs fresh mint - chopped
125 g (½ cup) scd yogurt

Combine all the ingredients in a small bowl and mix well. Serve chilled.

Mayonnaise

Makes 370 ml (1 ½ cups)

2 egg yolks
2 Tbs fresh lemon juice
2 Tbs water
1 tsp honey
1 tsp mustard powder
½ tsp salt
½ tsp white pepper
250 ml (1 cup) grapeseed oil or
sunflower oil

Fill a small pot a quarter of the way with hot water and bring to simmer. Place a heatproof bowl onto the pot. Add the egg yolks, lemon juice, water, honey, mustard, salt, pepper and whisk until the mixture thickens. Remove heat and pour into a food processor. Add a small amount of oil to the mixture and blend. While blending pour in a small amount of oil at a time until all the oil is blended and the mixture has thickened. Pour into a sealed jar and refrigerate. The mayonnaise will keep for up to 4 weeks in the refrigerator.

Sweet Condiments

Apple and Pear Sauce

Makes 1 liter (4 cups)

500 g (1 lb) Granny Smith apples
- peeled,
cored and chopped
1 kg (2 lb) pears - peeled, cored
and chopped
150 g (½ cup) honey
2 Tbs fresh lemon juice

Combine all ingredients in a heavy saucepan and simmer covered for 15 minutes. Uncover and stir. Cover and simmer for another 15 minutes. Take the lid off and cook for another 15 minutes. Pour the mixture into a food mixer and process until smooth. Refrigerate in an airtight jar.

Apricot Jam

Makes about 1 ½ cups

170 g (½ cup) dried apricots - chopped
120 ml (½ cup) boiling water
250 ml (1 cup) fresh orange juice
75 g (¼ cup) honey
250 ml (1 cup) water

Place the chopped apricots into a bowl with boiled water and let sit for 10 minutes, until the dried fruit has absorbed the water. Place into a small pot with the orange juice and honey, and bring to boil. Turn down the heat and simmer, adding the extra cup of water when needed. Cook for 50 - 60 minutes, until the jam has thickened. Add water as needed. Refrigerate in an airtight jar.

Blueberry Jam

Makes 1 cup

300 g (2 cups) blueberries
170 g (½ cup) honey
3 Tbs fresh orange juice

Combine all ingredients in a saucepan, cover and bring to a boil on medium heat. Simmer for 1 hour, stirring occasionally. The jam should be thick with a little juice simmering. Remove from stove and cool. Refrigerate in an airtight jar.

Custard Sauce

Serves 4

2 eggs - whole
1 egg yolk
250 g (1 cup) scd french cream^
75 g (¼ cup) honey

In a small pot combine the whole eggs, egg yolk and cream. Bring the heat up slowly, whisking constantly, avoiding boiling the cream. Once the cream^ has thickened, remove from heat and add honey, stirring until combined. Place the sauce in a jar and refrigerate for several hours before serving.

Honey Caramel Sauce

200 g (6 oz) butter
300 g (1 cup) honey

Place the butter and honey into a small saucepan on medium heat. Melt the butter and simmer for 5 minutes. Refrigerate in an airtight jar. The sauce will set in the refrigerator, but can be easily heated to liquefy.

Lemon Butter

Makes 2 cups

110 g (½ cup) butter - melted
170 g (½ cup) honey
250 g (1 cup) scd dripped yogurt^
pinch salt
1 Tbs fresh lemon juice
1 tsp lemon rind - grated
½ tsp vanilla essence*

*see essential ingredients list

Blend the butter and honey in a food processor until light and fluffy. Add the dripped yogurt, salt, lemon juice, rind, and vanilla and whip until the butter becomes quite fluffy. Refrigerate in an airtight jar for at least 4 hours.

Orange Caramel Sauce

Makes 1 cup

300 g (1 cup) honey
grated rind from 1 orange
2 Tbs fresh orange juice
200 g (6 oz) butter

Mix all ingredients into a small saucepan and simmer for 10 minutes. The sauce will harden when refrigerated, but can be heated up in the microwave to liquefy.

^All SCD yogurt items to be as per our home-made recipes.

Pink Grapefruit Crème Anglaise

3 egg yolks
4 Tbs honey
1 tsp vanilla essence*
250 g (1 cup) scd french cream^
120 ml (½ cup) fresh grapefruit juice

*see essential ingredients list

Fill a small pot a quarter of the way up with hot water and put onto medium heat. Simmer the water - do not boil it. Place a heatproof bowl onto the pot. Add the egg yolks and honey to the bowl and whisk until it thickens. Add the vanilla essence and whisk for another minute. Take off the heat and add the french cream^ and grapefruit juice and whisk until smooth. Let cool and serve.

Stewed Apples

Makes 300 g (6 cups)

300 g (10 oz) Granny Smith apples
- peeled, cored
½ lemon - juiced and grated rind
1 stick cinnamon
1 Tbs honey

Slice the apples into thick pieces and combine with all other ingredients in a saucepan. Cook covered for about 10 minutes or until apples have become quite soft. Refrigerate in an airtight jar.

Strawberry Jelly

Makes about 2 cups

375 g (2 ½ cups) fresh strawberries
- hulled and quartered
250 ml (1 cup) water
2 Tbs fresh lemon juice
150 g (½ cup) honey
1 Tbs gelatin
100 ml warm water

Place the strawberries, water, lemon juice, and honey into a medium saucepan. Bring to boil, then cover and simmer for 20 minutes. Remove from heat and strain through a sieve, gently squeezing out as much juice as possible. Dissolve the gelatin in 100 ml of warm water and stir into the hot juice. Pour into a glass jar, tighten lid and refrigerate overnight to set. Serve with our toasted light white bread or on our pancakes.

Strawberry Sauce

Makes 500 ml (2 cups)

300 g (2 cups) strawberries – hulled, chopped
150 g (½ cup) honey
60 ml (¼ cup) fresh orange juice

Place strawberries into a saucepan with the honey and fresh orange juice. Heat the strawberries until the liquid starts to simmer, and cook for about 10 minutes. Remove from heat and allow to cool. Place the mixture into a blender and blend until smooth. Refrigerate in an airtight jar.

Vanilla Custard

Serves 8 - 10

500 ml (2 cups) scd yogurt
500 ml (2 cups) scd french cream^
300 g (1 cup) honey
7 eggs - beaten
3 tsp vanilla essence*
¼ tsp salt

*see essential ingredients list

Preheat oven to 180°C/350°F

Combine the yogurt with the french cream^ and honey in a medium size pot, and heat on medium, stirring frequently. Shortly before reaching boiling point, remove from heat and add the beaten egg, vanilla essence, and salt. Pour the mixture into individual ramekins and place them into a deep baking dish. Fill the baking dish with water to half way up the ramekins. Bake the custard for 35 minutes. Remove from the oven and refrigerate for at least 3 hours. If using the custard as a thick sauce, remove the custard from the ramekins into a medium bowl and whisk until smooth.

Desserts

Almond and Raisin Custard

Makes 6

500 ml (2 cups) almond milk*
5 eggs - whisked
100 g (⅓ cup) honey
1 tsp vanilla essence**
50 g (¼ cup) raisins
6 strawberries

*see page 241 for recipe
**see essential ingredients list

Preheat the oven to 150°C/300°F

Combine the almond milk, eggs, honey and vanilla essence in a medium size pot and heat, whisking constantly. Do not boil. Cook for 1 minute, then remove from heat and pour into the ramekins. Evenly distribute the raisins amongst the ramekins. Place the ramekins in a heatproof dish filled with water reaching half way up the ramekins. Bake in the oven for 45 minutes or until the tops start to feel firm. Remove from the oven and place the custards into the refrigerator for at least 3 hours before serving. Decorate with slices of strawberries.

Strawberry and Fresh Fig Brulé

Serves 6

125 g (4 oz) very ripe figs* - sliced
125 g (4 oz) strawberries - hulled, sliced
750 g (3 cups) scd french cream^
5 eggs
75g (¼ cup) honey
1 tsp vanilla essence**
1 Tbs butter
75 g (¼ cup) honey

**see essential ingredients list

Preheat the oven to 180°C/370°F
6 x ¾ cup capacity ramekins

Place the fruit into the bottom and around the sides of the ramekins. Set aside.

Pour the french cream^ with the eggs, ¼ cup honey and vanilla essence into a medium pot and heat and whisk until well combined. Do not boil. Take off the heat and pour into the fruit filled ramekins. Place the ramekins into a deep baking dish, with water, which reaches half way up the ramekins. Bake for 35 – 40 minutes, until the custard has set. Refrigerate for at least 3 hours before serving. Before serving place the other ¼ cup of honey and butter into a small pot and bring to boil. Turn off heat the heat and let cool for 2 minutes. Dribble over the top of the dessert and serve.

* If figs are not available use fresh or frozen blueberries.

Photo: Almond and Raisin Custard

Apple and Blueberry Crumble

Serves 4

Filling

1.350 kg (2 lb 11 oz) Granny Smith
apples - peeled, diced and cored
200 g (1 cup) frozen blueberries
1 Tbs fresh orange juice
1 tsp lemon rind - grated
3 Tbs honey

Crumble

100 g (1 cup) almond flour
60 g (¼ cup) cold butter
1 tsp honey

Preheat oven to 150°C/300°F
Butter a 20 cm/8 inch square baking tin

Place all of the ingredients, retaining 2 Tbs of honey, in a medium size saucepan and cook covered on medium heat for 5 minutes. Remove lid and simmer on high for another 5 minutes. Drain the fruit of its juices in a sieve. Pour the juice back into the saucepan, adding the remaining tablespoon of honey, and simmer until reduced down by half. Retain this syrup for later. Cool the fruit in refrigerator.

Meanwhile, make the crumble by combining the almond flour, butter and honey in a food processor. Mix until chunky crumbs are formed. Place the crumble in the refrigerator for 10 minutes.

When the fruit has cooled down, place it into the prepared baking tin and top with the crumble.

Bake for 30 minutes or until crumble is golden brown. Serve warm, topped with a little french cream or scd yogurt and the retained syrup.

Cherry Crumble

Serves 4

150 g (1 ½ cups) almond flour
1 Tbs honey
60 g (¼ cup) dripped scd yogurt^
60 g (¼ cup) butter - cold, diced small
70 g (½ cup) apricot jam*
40 g (1 cup) flaked coconut**
120 g (¾ cup) dried cherries**

*see page 156 for recipe
**if unsweetened dried cherries can't be found substitute with sulphur free dried apricots.

Preheat the oven to 170°C/340°F
Line a baking tray with baking paper

Combine the almond flour with the honey, dripped yogurt^, and butter. Knead the butter through the dough. Don't worry if some of the small chunks of butter do not mix completely. Refrigerate the dough, covered for 1 hour. Remove from refrigerator and divide dough in half. Roll out two 30 x 20 cm/12 x 8 inch rectangles by placing the dough between 2 sheets of baking paper. Remove the top layer of baking paper. Spread half the jam, coconut, and cherries on each rectangle. Using the bottom layer of the baking paper, roll the dough into a log and gently place onto the lined baking tray. Bake in the oven for 45 minutes, or until the logs start to brown. Remove from the oven and let cool for ½ hour. Cut each log in half and serve with our custard sauce.

Banana Ice Cream with Strawberry Sauce

Serves 6

5 ripe bananas
300 g (1 cup) honey
120 ml (½ cup) scd french cream^
500 g (2 cups) scd yogurt^
2 tsp vanilla essence*

*see essential ingredients list

Peel bananas and place into a blender with the honey, french cream^, yogurt^ and vanilla essence. Blend until smooth. Pour into a sealable plastic container and freeze overnight. Serve with fresh strawberries and our strawberry sauce.

Vanilla Ice Cream

Serves 8

300 g (4 whole) frozen bananas
170 g (½ cup) honey
250 g (1 cup) scd yogurt^
250 ml (1 cup) scd french cream^
15 ml (1 Tbs) vanilla essence*

*see essential ingredients list

Chop the bananas and combine with all ingredients in a food processor and process until smooth. If you have an ice-cream maker, pour the mixture into the ice-cream maker and churn for 20 minutes. Otherwise, pour mixture into a plastic container and freeze for about 2 hours before serving.

Very Berry Ice Cream

Serves 8

300 g (2 cups) frozen mixed berries
170 g (½ cup) honey
500 g (2 cups) scd yogurt^
15 ml (1 Tbs) fresh lemon juice

Combine all ingredients in a food processor and process until smooth. If you have an ice-cream maker, pour the mixture into the ice-cream maker and churn for 20 minutes. Otherwise, pour mixture into a plastic container and freeze for about 2 hours before serving.

Photo: Banana Ice Cream with Strawberry Sauce

Blanc Manger

2 Tbs gelatin
3 Tbs water
500 g (2 cups) scd french cream^
180 ml (¾ cup) cherry or grape juice*
150 g (½ cup) honey
70 g (¾ cup) almond flour
250 ml (1 cup) water
1 tsp vanilla essence*
90 g (3 oz) cherries – pitted, halved**

*see essential ingredients list
****any kind of soft flesh fruit can be
   used (i.e. raspberries, mangoes)**

One 23 cm/9 inch round cake mould

Place the gelatin into a small bowl with water and combine. When soft and spongy place the gelatin into the microwave and heat for 15 seconds to liquefy. Set aside to cool in the refrigerator for 10 minutes.

Whip the french cream^ until it holds medium to firm peaks. Set aside in the refrigerator.

Pour the fruit juice into a medium saucepan with the honey and almond flour, and bring to a boil, stirring until the honey is dissolved. Remove from heat and stir in the dissolved gelatin and vanilla essence.

Retrieve the cream from the refrigerator. Combine the fruit juice mixture with the cream, folding it under with a flexible rubber spatula. Lightly fold under the cherries. Pour the mixture into a non-stick mould and refrigerate overnight.

To remove blanc manger, dip the mould into some warm water for a few seconds to loosen the blanc manger and tip onto a flat serving plate. Serve cold, decorated with fresh fruit.

Exotic Fruit Flan

Serves 4

4 eggs
2 egg yolks
100 g (⅓ cup) honey
juice from 1 lemon
250 ml (1 cup) scd french cream^
350 g (11 oz) raspberries
2 kiwi fruit - peeled, sliced
70 g (½ cup) strawberries - hulled, sliced

Preheat oven to 180°C/360°F
Lightly oil 4 ramekins

In a small bowl combine eggs, egg yolks and honey, and whip until creamy. Add the lemon juice and stir well. Pour in the french cream^ and mix until thoroughly combined. Distribute the raspberries into the bottom of the 4 ramekins. Pour over the batter. Place ramekins into a large baking tray and fill hot water half way up the ramekins. Bake the flans for 20 minutes or until you can feel they are firming up when pressed lightly. Turn off oven and carefully remove the ramekins from the oven tray. Cool for at least 4 hours in refrigerator before serving. To serve, place the ramekins into hot water for 20 seconds and invert onto a plate. Place fruit in a decorative manner on top of the flan. It is not necessary to remove the flans from the ramekins. They will look just as spectacular served with the fruit on top.

Photo: Exotic Fruit Flan

Blueberry Pie

Serves 6-8

Pie Shell

300 g (3 cups) almond flour
½ tsp baking soda
¼ tsp salt
50 g (2 oz) butter - cold, diced small
2 Tbs honey
1 egg

Filling

1 kg (2 lb) frozen blueberries
700 g (1.5 lb) Granny Smith apples
- peeled, cored, diced
80 ml (⅓ cup) fresh lemon juice
225 g (¾ cup) honey

1 egg yolk

Preheat the oven to 150°C/300°F
Butter a 23 cm/9 inch round pie dish

Combine the almond flour with the baking soda and salt. Add the butter, honey, and egg and knead until well combined. Some of the butter will still show in the dough and that is fine. Flatten the dough and refrigerate for 30 minutes. Remove from refrigerator, returning one third of the dough back into the fridge for later. Roll out the dough between two sheets of baking paper until big enough to cover the pie dish. Press into the prepared pie dish and bake for 20 minutes until the crust is golden brown. Turn off the oven and let the crust cool in the oven until completely cool.

Meanwhile, make the filling by combining the blueberries with the apples, lemon juice, and honey in a large pot and bring to boil. Reduce the heat and cook uncovered for 20 minutes or until the liquid has thickened. Remove from heat and place in a covered bowl in the refrigerator. Let cool and set for at least 3 - 4 hours or overnight. Once set, fill the pie crust with the mixture. Roll out the rest of the dough and cover the pie. Brush the top with the whipped egg yolk and bake for 15 minutes on 180°C/370°F until the top has turned golden brown. Remove from oven and either serve warm or let set in the fridge and serve cold with our custard sauce or a little french cream.

Cherry Clafouti

Serves 8

4 eggs
150 g (½ cup) honey
1 tsp vanilla essence*
180 ml (¾ cup) scd french cream^
250 g (2 ½ cups) almond flour
1 tsp baking soda
450 g (1 ¾ cups) cherries - pitted

*see essential ingredients list

Preheat oven to 170°C/340°F
Line a 20 cm/8 inch square cake tin with baking paper

Beat the eggs, honey and vanilla essence until light and fluffy. Add the french cream^ and mix well. Combine the almond flour with the baking soda and fold under the egg mixture. Distribute the cherries evenly into the bottom of the baking tin. Pour the batter over the cherries. Bake for 1 hour until the cake feels spongy when pressed. Let cool before removing from the tin. Tip the tin carefully onto a serving plate and gently peel off the baking paper. Serve with french cream^.

Lemon Meringue Pie

Serves 8

Pie Shell

200 g (2 cups) almond flour
½ tsp baking soda
¼ tsp salt
30 g (1 oz) butter - cold, diced small
2 Tbs honey

Lemon Filling

6 egg yolks - save egg whites
300 g (1 cup) honey
110 g (½ cup) butter - diced
120 ml (½ cup) fresh lemon juice

Meringue

6 egg whites
75 g (⅓ cup) honey

Preheat the oven to 150°C/300°F
Butter a 23 cm/9 inch round pie dish

Combine the almond flour with the baking soda and salt. Add the butter and honey and knead to combine. Do not worry if some of the butter still shows in the dough. Form the dough into a flat disk and refrigerate for 30 minutes. Remove from the refrigerator and place between two sheets of baking paper. Roll the dough out to a round disk a little larger than the pie dish. Remove the top sheet and invert onto the pie dish. With your hands, mould the dough to fit the pie dish, making the edges a little thicker. Place into the oven and bake for 20 minutes until the crust has browned slightly and is firm. Remove from oven and cool completely.

Meanwhile, prepare the filling by placing a heatproof bowl over a pot filled a quarter of the way with water. Bring to boil, then reduce heat to a simmer. Add egg yolks and honey to the bowl and whisk until well combined. Then add a chunk of butter at a time, whisking constantly. Add the next chunk when the previous one has melted. This will take about 15 minutes. It helps to use an electric mixer on slow to keep mixing constantly. Keep mixing until all butter is used and the filling has thickened. Add lemon juice and keep mixing for another minute. Remove from heat and let cool in the refrigerator while you prepare the meringue.

Beat the egg whites until stiff, add the honey, and keep beating until shiny and firm.

Take the lemon filling from the fridge and spread on to the cooled pie crust. Then top with the egg white, forming decorative peaks across the top.

Bake in the oven on 200°C/390°F for about 5-10 minutes until the top of the peaks have turned a nice gold brown.

Photo: Lemon Meringue Pie

Grape Juice Jelly

Serves 4

500 ml (2 cups) grape juice*
1 Tbs gelatin

***see essential ingredients list**

Take 80 ml/⅓ cup of the grape juice, pour into a small bowl, and dissolve the gelatin until thick and spongy. Heat the rest of the juice in a saucepan until just boiling. Turn off the heat and pour in the gelatin and whisk until all the gelatin has dissolved. Pour into individual jelly moulds or small bowls and refrigerate for 4 hours or until set.

Any pure juice can be used for this recipe. If using unsweetened cranberry juice, add 1 Tbs of honey to sweeten.

Pavlova

Makes 6

4 egg whites
150 g (½ cup) honey
200 g (3 ½ cups) flaked coconut*

Topping
160 ml (⅔ cup) scd french cream^
2 Tbs honey
1 tsp vanilla essence*
85 g (½ cup) raspberries
1 kiwi fruit – peeled and sliced

*see essential ingredients list

Preheat oven to 140°C/280°F
Line a baking tray with baking paper

Whip egg whites until stiff. Add the honey and keep whipping until it is thick and creamy. Carefully fold under the coconut. Place large dollops of the mixture onto the prepared baking tray. Bake the meringues for 1 hour or until they start to brown. Let cool in oven with the door slightly ajar. When cooled, remove and add topping.

Whip the french cream^ with the honey and vanilla until stiff. Place two large tablespoonfuls of the mix on top of the meringues and decorate with the fresh fruit.

^All SCD yogurt items to be as per our home-made recipes.

Photo: Pavlova

Orange Mousse

Makes 6

225 g (¾ cup) honey
grated rind from 1 orange
60 ml (¼ cup) cold water
1 tsp gelatin
2 Tbs cold water
160 ml (⅔ cup) fresh orange juice
2 Tbs lemon juice
370 ml (1 ½ cups) scd french cream^
½ tsp nutmeg
½ tsp cinnamon

Heat the honey and orange rind and 60ml/¼ cup cold water in a small saucepan and simmer for 1 minute. Turn off the heat. In a small bowl soak the gelatin in the 2 Tbs of cold water and add to the hot honey stirring well. Pour into a ceramic bowl and refrigerate about 20 minutes until it starts to thicken. Remove from refrigerator. Whip the french cream^ until quite thick. Combine well with the orange juice, lemon juice and thickened honey. Pour the mixture into 6 small ramekins and refrigerate for at least 4 hours. When firm, dip the ramekins into hot water for about 10 seconds. With a knife, separate the edges of the mousse from the ramekin and place upside down onto the centre of a dessert plate. Remove the ramekin and decorate with the nutmeg and honey and with some slivers of candied orange peel. Add orange caramel sauce if desired.

Candied Orange Peel

Makes 1 cup

3 oranges
300 g (1 cup) honey
120 ml (½ cup) water

Cut off both ends of the orange and slice into the peel lengthwise. Peel off the skin and use oranges for juicing for above recipe. Cut the peel into 5 mm/¼ inch thick slices. Place the peel into a small pot of water and bring to boil. Drain the water and repeat the boiling and draining process 3 times in all. In another pot, bring the honey and ½ cup of water to boil. Turn down the heat and simmer for 10 minutes. Add the peel and simmer for 40 minutes until the orange peel turns translucent. Drain off the honey and reserve for use in the Orange Caramel Sauce recipe.

Orange Caramel Sauce

Makes 1 cup

300 g (1 cup) honey
grated rind from 1 orange
2 Tbs fresh orange juice
200 g butter

If using the retained honey from the above recipe, simply add enough honey to make 1 cup, and eliminate the orange rind. Otherwise, mix all ingredients into a small saucepan and simmer for 10 minutes. The sauce will harden when refrigerated, but can be heated in the microwave to liquefy.

Poached Pears
in Honey Orange Glaze

Makes 4

4 firm pears - peeled
250 ml (1 cup) water
10 cm orange peel
2 Tbs fresh orange juice
150 g (½ cup) honey

Place the whole pears with stems intact into a medium size saucepan. Add the water, orange peel, juice, and honey. Bring to boil, and then reduce heat and simmer covered for 20 minutes. Let cool and serve either warm or cold with scd french cream, dividing the leftover juice amongst them. Cut the orange peel into four strips and decorate the pears with them.

Pear and Almond Pudding

Serves 6

100 g (3 oz) butter – room temperature
150 g (½ cup) honey
150 g (1 ½ cups) almond flour
1 tsp vanilla essence*
1 whole egg
3 eggs - separated
2 pears – peeled, cored and finely chopped

Crème Anglaise

3 egg yolks
4 Tbs honey
1 tsp vanilla essence*
250 g (1 cup) scd french cream^
120 ml (½ cup) fresh grapefruit juice

Preheat the oven to 180˚C/370˚F
Lightly butter 6 x ¾ cup capacity ramekins

Beat the butter with half the honey until creamy. Beat in the almond flour, vanilla essence, the whole egg and the three egg yolks. Fold in the pears. In another bowl, whisk the egg whites until they stiffen. Add the rest of the honey and whisk until thick and creamy. Fold under the almond mixture. Spoon the mixture into the ramekins and place onto an oven tray. Bake in the oven for 25 – 30 minutes, or until the puddings feel spongy. Take out of the oven and let cool for 10 minutes. Then turn out onto serving plates. Serve with the pink grapefruit crème anglaise.

To make the sauce place a small pot, filling it with hot water quarter of the way up, onto medium heat. Simmer the water and do not boil it. Place a heat proof dish onto the pot. Add the egg yolks and honey to the bowl and whisk until it thickens. Add the vanilla essence and whisk for another minute. Take off the heat and add the french cream^ and grapefruit juice and whisk until smooth. Let cool and serve with the puddings.

Pink Grapefruit Crème Anglaise

3 egg yolks
4 Tbs honey
1 tsp vanilla essence*
250 g (1 cup) scd french cream^
120 ml (½ cup) fresh grapefruit juice

*see essential ingredients list

Fill a small pot a quarter of the way up with hot water and put onto medium heat. Simmer the water - do not boil it. Place a heatproof bowl onto the pot. Add the egg yolks and honey to the bowl and whisk until it thickens. Add the vanilla essence and whisk for another minute. Take off the heat and add the french cream^ and grapefruit juice and whisk until smooth. Let cool and serve.

Sticky Date Pudding

Serves 8

200 g (1 ½ cups) pitted dates*
80 ml (⅓ cup) boiling water
100 g (3 oz) butter - softened
150 g (½ cup) honey
3 eggs
80 g (⅓ cup) scd yogurt^
250 g (2 ½ cups) almond flour
1 ½ tsp baking soda

Caramel Sauce
200 g (6 oz) butter
300 g (1 cup) honey

***see essential ingredients list under dried fruit**

Preheat oven to 150°C/300°F
Line a 20 cm/8 inch square cake tin with baking paper

Place the dates and boiling water in a food processor and process until dates are chopped. In a bowl mix the butter and honey until creamy. Add the eggs gradually and beat well. Pour this mixture into the chopped dates with the yogurt^ and blend. Mix the almond flour and baking soda together and combine with the date mixture. Pour the mixture into the cake tin and bake for 60 minutes, or until the cake feels spongy.

To make the honey caramel sauce, place the butter and honey in a saucepan and over medium heat simmer for 10 minutes. The sauce will harden when kept in the refrigerator. Heat up in the microwave before serving.

Serve the sticky date pudding warm with scd french cream^, strawberries and the warm honey caramel sauce.

Photo: Sticky Date Pudding

Raspberry Soufflé

Serves 4

500 g (2 cups) scd dripped yogurt^
3 eggs – separated
1 egg – whole
100 g (⅓ cup) honey
1 Tbs lemon rind - grated
150 g (1 ⅓ cup) raspberries

Preheat the oven to 180°C/360°F
Butter 4 x 1 cup ramekins

Place the dripped yogurt, 3 egg yolks, 1 whole egg , honey and lemon rind into a large bowl and mix well. Fold under the raspberries. In another bowl, whisk the egg whites until they form stiff peaks. Gently fold the egg whites under the yogurt mixture and distribute evenly amongst the 4 ramekins. Bake the soufflés for 25 minutes or until they have risen and have turned golden. Garnish with fresh raspberries and serve with a little scd french cream^.

Strawberry, Rhubarb and Lime Tarts

Makes 6

Pastry

200 g (2 cups) almond flour
120 g (½ cup) butter - cold, diced small
1 tsp vanilla essence*
1 Tbs grated lime rind

Filling

140 g (1 cup) strawberries - hulled and chopped
140 g (1 cup) rhubarb - chopped
3 Tbs honey
30 g (½ cup) desiccated coconut*
120 g (½ cup) scd dripped yogurtˆ
1 Tbs grated lime rind

*see essential ingredients list

Preheat the oven to 150°C/300°F
Line an oven tray with baking paper

Combine all the ingredients for the pastry and knead until well combined. Some of the butter might still show through, that is fine. Flatten into a disk and refrigerate covered for 1 hour.

Meanwhile combine the strawberries, rhubarb, honey, and coconut. In another bowl, combine the dripped yogurtˆ with the lemon rind.

Take the dough from the refrigerator and separate into 6 equal parts, shaping them into large patties. Place on top of the lined baking tray and press into the centre of each patty to create a large hollow. Add about 1 tablespoon of the dripped yogurtˆ and lime mixture into the bottom of the hollow. Then top with the fruit mixture. Mold the dough to form around the edges of the fruit mixture. Place into the oven and bake for 40 minutes. Take out of the oven and let cool completely before serving.

These tarts are delicious with our custard sauce, or a dollop of scd french creamˆ.

Zabaglione and Strawberries

Serves 4

500 g (1 lb) strawberries
60 ml (¼ cup) fresh orange juice
1Tbs honey

4 egg yolks
75 g (¼ cup) honey
120 ml (½ cup) dry white wine*

***see essential ingredients list**

Wash and hull strawberries. Slice in half and place into a pot with the orange juice and honey. Simmer for 3 minutes. Remove from heat and let cool.

Place the 4 egg yolks, honey and wine in a heatproof bowl over a saucepan filled a quarter way up with water and bring to a simmer on medium heat. Whisk either by hand or with an electric beater until thick and forming ribbon-like trails. Remove from heat and beat for 1 minute.

Place the strawberries into a glass and top with a generous amount of the zabaglione.

Breads
Cakes
Muffins
Biscuits

Almond Crescent Biscuits

Makes 30

3 egg whites
1 tsp vanilla essence*
170 g (½ cup) honey
300 g (3 cups) almond flour
100 g (1 cup) slivered almonds

*see essential ingredients list

Preheat oven to 170°C/340°F
Line two baking trays with baking paper

Place the egg whites into a medium bowl and whisk until bubbles form. Add the vanilla essence and honey and whisk again until thick and creamy. Fold into the almond flour and mix to form a thick paste. With moist hands form 1 cm/½ inch thick rolls about 8 cm/3 inches long. Then roll them in the almond slivers. Place onto the baking tray and form into a crescent. Bake the biscuits for 30 minutes or until they start to brown lightly. Cool completely and store in an airtight container.

Brownies

Makes 9

150 g (½ cup) honey
100 g (¾ cup) pitted dates* - chopped
75 g (¾ cup) almond flour
1 tsp baking soda
1 tsp fresh lemon juice
125 g butter – softened
2 eggs - beaten
50 g (2 oz) pecan nuts - crushed
¼ tsp salt

Preheat oven to 150°C/300°F
Line a 20 cm/8 inch square cake tin with baking paper

Place the honey in a medium pot and heat on medium. Add the dates, almond flour, baking soda and lemon juice and stir. Then add the butter and when melted add the beaten eggs, pecan nuts, salt, and combine well. Remove from heat and pour mixture into the prepared cake tin and bake for 30 minutes, or until the cake feels firm.

Remove the cake from oven and let cool for 10 minutes. Cut into 9 squares. Let cool completely and store in the refrigerator in an airtight container.

*see essential ingredients list under dried fruitt

Photo: Almond Crescent Biscuits and Coconut Date Balls

Apple and Cinnamon Muffins

Makes 6

2 eggs - separated
1 whole egg
60 g (¼ cup) butter - softened
60 g (¼ cup) scd yogurt^
150 g (½ cup) honey
250 g (2 ½ cups) almond flour
½ tsp ground cinnamon
1 tsp baking soda
225 g (1 cup) Granny Smith apples
- peeled,
cored and chopped

Preheat oven to 150°C/300°F
Butter large 6-hole muffin tin

Place the two egg yolks and the one whole egg into a large bowl. Add butter, yogurt^, honey, and whisk or beat with an electric mixer until light and fluffy. In another bowl, combine the almond flour, cinnamon, and baking soda. Whisk the egg whites in another bowl until stiff peaks form. Pour the almond flour mixture into the previously combined egg and yogurt mixture and combine well. Add the apple and egg white and gently fold under. Pour the batter into the buttered muffin tin and bake for 40 minutes until muffins feel spongy when pressed.

Leave to cool. Store in an airtight container.

Biscotti

Makes 36

120 g (½ cup) butter - softened
225 g (¾ cup) honey
2 large eggs
1 tsp vanilla essence*
350 g (3 ½ cups) almond flour
2 tsp ground cinnamon
2 tsp ground anise seeds
1 tsp baking soda
½ tsp salt
110 g (1 cup) slivered almonds
100 g (½ cup) currants
55 g (½ cup) pistachio nuts - crushed

*see essential ingredients list

Preheat oven to 150°C/300°F
Line two 21 x10 cm/8 x 4 inch loaf tins with baking paper

In a large bowl combine butter and honey and beat until creamy. Add the eggs, vanilla, and mix well. In another bowl, combine almond flour, cinnamon, anise seeds, baking soda, salt, nuts, and dried fruit. Mix the dry ingredients into the butter mixture and blend well.

Pour the batter into the prepared loaf tins. Gather the paper above the dough and fold lengthwise. This will pull the dough together and give it a more round log shape when baked. Bake for 40-50 minutes or until the dough is quite firm. Remove from the oven and let cool slightly. Take the baked biscotti logs from the loaf tins and unwrap. With a sharp knife cut the logs into thin slices. Line a baking tray with baking paper and place the slices back into the oven and bake for 15 minutes on each side, turning them over when one side has baked for its given time. For extra crispness leave the biscotti slices in the oven, after it has been turned off, until cooled down. Store them in an airtight container.

Photo: Biscotti and Chai Tea

Blueberry Cheesecake

Serves 4

Base

250 g (2 ½ cups) almond flour
100 g (¹/₃ cup) butter
1 tsp honey

Filling

2 Tbs gelatin
60 ml (¼ cup) tepid water
500 g (2 cups) drained scd yogurt^
150 g (½ cup) honey
80 ml (¹/₃ cup) fresh lemon juice
370 ml (1 ½ cups) scd french cream^

Topping

250 g (1 ½ cups) frozen blueberries
60 ml (¼ cup) water
2 Tbs honey

Pre-heat oven to 150°C/300°F
Butter a 20 cm/8 inch round spring form tin

To make the base, combine cold butter, honey, and almond flour and knead into a firm dough. Refrigerate for 30 minutes then remove and roll out between two sheets of baking paper. Then press the dough into the prepared spring-form tin. Bake until the base is golden brown, about 30 minutes. Remove from the oven and let cool completely.

Add the gelatin to the 60 ml/¼ cup of tepid water in a heatproof bowl, mix and let it go spongy. Bring about 4 cm/1 ½ inches of water to boil in a pot. Take the pot from the oven and place the heatproof bowl with gelatin into the water. Stir until the gelatin has dissolved. Take from the heat and set aside. Alternatively place the spongy gelatin into the microwave for 15 seconds.

To make the filling, combine drained yogurt^, honey and lemon juice in a food processor and process until smooth. Scrape into a bowl and add the french cream^ and half of the gelatin and mix. Set aside.

Place the frozen blueberries into a pot. Add 60 ml/¼ cup of water and add 2 tablespoons of honey and cook on low heat, about 15 minutes, until berries have softened. Place them into a food strainer and squeeze out all of the juice. Discard the pulp and add the other half of the gelatin to the juice and combine well. Set aside and allow to cool.

Pour the cream filling into the base, then pour the blueberry sauce on top. With the handle of a spoon start a snail trail from the centre out at an angle pushing the blueberry sauce into the cream filling.

Let it cool in refrigerator for at least 4 hours before serving.

Carrot Cake with Cream Cheese Icing

Makes 1 Loaf

4 eggs
80 g (⅓ cup) butter – softened
150 g (½ cup) honey
60 g (¼ cup) apple & pear sauce*
250 g (2 cups) carrots – peeled, grated
60 g (⅓ cup) dried apricots**
– chopped
250 g (2 ½ cups) almond flour
1 tsp cinnamon
2 tsp baking soda
¼ tsp salt

Icing

120 g (½ cup) scd dripped yogurt^
3 Tbs honey
1 tsp vanilla essence**

*see page 156 for recipe
**see essential ingredients list

Preheat the oven to 150˚C/300˚F
Line a 10 x 21 cm/4 x 8 inch loaf tin with baking paper

Whisk together the eggs, butter, honey, apple, and pear sauce until creamy. Add the carrots and apricots and blend. Combine the almond flour with the cinnamon, baking soda and salt and blend with the egg mixture. Pour the batter into the prepared loaf tin and bake for 70 minutes until the top of the loaf feels firm and spongy. Remove from the oven and let cool completely. When cooled down place the icing ingredients into a bowl and mix well. Spread the icing evenly over the top of the cake and refrigerate.

This is a wonderfully moist cake and the apricots are optional. If no applesauce is available, one banana will do just as good a job.

Photo: Carrot Cake with Cream Cheese Icing

Chewy Macadamia Nut Biscuits

Makes about 30

400 g (4 cups) almond flour
1 tsp baking soda
1 egg
1 tsp vanilla essence*
300 g (1 cup) honey
60 g (½ cup) macadamias -
chopped roughly
110 g (1 cup) dates - chopped roughly**
60 g (1 cup) shredded coconut*

*see essential ingredients list
**see essential ingredients list under
dried fruit

Preheat the oven to 150°C/300°F
Line a baking tray with baking paper

Combine the almond flour with the baking soda. In another bowl, whisk the egg with the vanilla essence and honey. Combine with the almond flour and add the macadamias, dates, and coconut. With moist hands shape the dough into ping-pong sized balls and flatten when placing onto the lined baking tray, leaving enough room for expansion. Bake for about 15 - 20 minutes until the biscuits have turned a golden brown color. Cool and store in an airtight jar.

Ginger Bear Biscuits

Makes about 40

500 g (5 cups) almond flour
1 tsp baking soda
200 g (⅔ cup) honey
100 g (⅓ cup) dark honey
30 g (1 oz) scd yogurt^
1 egg
2 Tbs ground cinnamon
2 Tbs ground ginger
2 Tbs ground cloves

Preheat the oven to 150°C/300°F
Line a baking tray with baking paper

Combine the almond flour with the baking soda. In another bowl, mix the honey, dark honey, yogurt^, egg, and spices together. Then combine with the almond flour and knead into firm dough. Refrigerate covered for at least 2 hours. Take out the dough and roll out the dough until about 2 mm thick. Take a bear shaped biscuit cutter and dip in cold water and cut out as many shapes as possible. Gather the left over dough and refrigerate until ready to use for the second batch. Place all the bears onto the lined baking tray and bake for 15 minutes. Take out of the oven and turn biscuits over. Place back into the oven and bake for another 5 - 10 minutes, making sure biscuits do not brown too much. Let biscuits cool completely before storing in an airtight jar.

Hazelnut Rounds

Makes about 20

80 g (⅓ cup) butter - softened
200 g (⅔ cup) honey
3 eggs
250 g (2 ½ cups) almond flour
250 g (2 ½ cups) hazelnut meal
¼ tsp ground cardamom
¼ tsp ground cloves
¼ tsp ground ginger
1 tsp lemon rind - grated

Preheat the oven to 150°C/300°F
Line a baking tray with baking paper

Combine the butter, honey, eggs, and mix until creamy. In another bowl, combine the almond flour, hazelnut meal, spices, and lemon rind. Mix into the butter mixture until smooth. Spread the dough onto the baking tray about 5 mm thick. Bake for 20 minutes. Remove from the oven and let cool for about 10 minutes. With a round cookie cutter cut out as many shapes as possible. Store in an airtight container.

Christmas Pudding

Serves 8 - 10

200 g (1 cup) dried dates*
200 g (1 cup) dried figs*
200 g (1 cup) dried prunes*
120 ml (½ cup) boiling water
100 g (1 cup) pecans
100 g (1 cup) blanched almonds
250 ml (1 cup) grape juice*
60 ml (¼ cup) fresh orange juice
120 ml (½ cup) bourbon
2 egg yolks
200 g (1 cup) sultanas
1 Tbs grated orange rind
200 g (2 cups) almond flour
½ tsp ground cinnamon
¼ tsp ground cloves
¼ tsp ground nutmeg

*see essential ingredients list

Place the dried dates, figs, prunes, hot water, pecans, almonds, grape juice, orange juice, bourbon and egg yolk into a food processor and process the mixture until chopped and well combined. Remove from the processor into a large bowl and add the sultanas, orange rind, almond flour, and spices. Mix well and then pour the dough into a 1 - 1 ½ liter/2 ½ pint pudding dish. Cover the dish well with baking paper and foil. Place into a large pot with water so the level reaches ²/₃ of the way up the pudding dish. Cover and steam for 6 hours. Add more water as required, to maintain level. Remove from the heat and let cool for 10 minutes. Then remove pudding and either serve immediately with custard, or freeze for up to six weeks. Pudding can be reheated the next day, as well, in the oven or microwave.

Custard

Serves 8 - 10

500 ml (2 cups) scd yogurt^
500 ml (2 cups) scd french cream^
300 g (1 cup) honey
7 eggs - beaten
3 tsp vanilla essence*
¼ tsp salt

*see essential ingredients list

Preheat oven to 180°C/350°F

In a medium sized pot combine the yogurt^ with the french cream^ and honey and heat on medium, stirring frequently. Do not boil, but short before reaching boiling point, turn off the heat and add the beaten eggs, vanilla essence, and salt. Pour the mixture into individual ramekins and place them into a deep baking dish. Fill the baking dish with water to reach half way up the ramekins. Bake the custard for 35 minutes. Remove from the oven and refrigerate for at least 3 hours. If using the custard as a thick sauce, remove the custard from the ramekins into a medium bowl and whisk until smooth.

Photo: Christmas Pudding with Custard

Lemon Tarts

Makes 10

Tart Shells

200 g (2 cups) almond flour
½ tsp baking soda
¼ tsp salt
30 g butter – cold, diced small
2 Tbs honey

Lemon Filling

6 egg yolks
225 g (¾ cup) honey
120 ml (½ cup) fresh lemon juice
110 g (½ cup) butter – diced
1 Tbs grated lemon rind

Preheat the oven to 200°C/390°F
Lightly oil 10 aluminum tart moulds

Combine the almond flour with the baking soda and salt. Add the butter and honey and knead to combine. Do not worry if some of the butter still shows in the dough. Form the dough into a flat disk and refrigerate for 30 minutes. Then take the dough from the refrigerator and place between two sheets of baking paper. Roll the dough out thin, about 3 mm/⅛ inch thick. Cut out rounds, slightly larger than the tart moulds and mould the dough into the shells. Place onto a baking tray and bake in the oven for about 15-20 minutes, until they are baked through and slightly brown. Remove from the oven and let cool completely.

Meanwhile prepare the filling by placing a heatproof bowl over the top of a pot filled a quarter of the way up with water. Bring to boil then turn down the heat to a simmer. Whisk the egg yolks and honey in the bowl until well combined. Then add one chunk of butter at a time, whisking constantly. Add the next chunk when the first has melted. Add lemon juice and rind and keep mixing. This will take about 15 minutes and it helps to use an electric mixer on slow to keep mixing constantly. Keep mixing once all the butter has been used until the filling has thickened. Remove from the heat and let cool down to room temperature. Then fill the cooled down tart shells and place in the refrigerator to set. Refrigerate in a covered container.

Lemon Drop Biscuits

Makes 30

170 g (¾ cup) butter – room temperature
200 g (⅔ cup) honey
300 g (3 cups) almond flour
2 tsp vanilla essence*
1 Tbs grated lemon rind

*see essential ingredients list

Preheat the grill to 150°C/300°F
Line a baking tray with baking paper.

Beat butter and honey until creamy. Add the almond flour, vanilla essence, and lemon rind and combine well. With moist hands take 1 tsp full of dough and form into a ball. Place on the prepared baking tray and leave about 5 cm/2 inches between each ball. Bake for 10 – 15 minutes. The biscuits should only be lightly browned. Remove from the oven and let cool completely. Store in an airtight container.

Lemon-Yogurt Cake

Serves 8

4 eggs – separated
150 g (½ cup) honey
2 tsp vanilla essence*
500 ml (2 cups) scd yogurt^
rind and juice of 1 lemon
200 g (2 cups) almond flour
2 tsp baking soda

*see essential ingredients list

Preheat the oven to 150°C/300°F
Line a 20 cm (8 inch) square baking tin with baking paper

Combine the egg yolk with the honey, vanilla essence, yogurt^, lemon rind, lemon juice and mix well. Combine the almond flour with the baking soda and add to the egg yolk mixture. Beat the egg whites until stiff and gently fold under. Pour the mixture into the prepared cake tin and bake for 1 hour, or until the cake feels spongy. Let cool before removing from the tin. Serve with fresh fruit and SCD french cream.

Pink Grapefruit and Orange Cake

Serves 8

1 medium navel orange
1 lemon
1 mandarin
250 g (¾ cup) honey
6 eggs
250 (2 ½ cups) almond flour
1 tsp baking soda

Syrup
250 g (¾ cup) honey
120 ml (½ cup) fresh pink
grapefruit juice
120 ml (½ cup) fresh orange juice
Rind from 1 orange and 1 pink
grapefruit

Preheat oven to 170˚C/340˚F
Butter a 23 cm/9 inch round cake tin or line a 20 cm/8 inch square cake tin with baking paper.

Place the whole orange, whole lemon and whole mandarin in a saucepan and cover with cold water. Bring to a boil and simmer for 45 minutes or until fruit becomes soft. Check water level and add more if needed. Remove from water and cool. Slice open and remove seeds. Puree in a blender. In the meantime, beat honey and eggs until light and fluffy. Fold through the pureed fruit. In another bowl, mix the almond flour and baking soda and then fold through the egg and fruit mixture. Pour mixture into the prepared baking tin and bake in the oven for 1 hour. The cake is done when the top feels spongy when pressed. Remove from oven and cool before removing from the tin.

Prepare the syrup by placing the honey, grapefruit juice, and orange juice into a small saucepan. Chop the rind into thin slivers and add to the juice. Bring to a boil and then simmer for about 10 minutes until the rind looks translucent.

Remove the rind and decorate the top of the cake with it. Pour the syrup over the top and serve with SCD french cream^.

Pumpernickel Bread

Makes 1 Loaf

120 g (1 cup) walnuts
30 g (¼ cup) sunflower seeds
400 g (4 cups) almond flour
½ tsp salt
1 tsp baking soda
3 eggs
80 g (⅓ cup) butter
1 tsp honey

Preheat the oven to 150°C/300°F
Line a 10 x 21 cm/4 x 8 inch loaf tin with baking paper

Place walnuts and sunflower seeds into a food processor chop nuts for 5 seconds with the sharp blade inserted. Take out the sharp blade and insert mixing blade. Add almond flour, salt and baking soda and mix. In another bowl, whisk the eggs, butter, and honey until fluffy. Pour into food processor and process with the almond flour until the dough is well combined. The dough will be quite thick and heavy. Pour the dough into the lined loaf tin and bake for 1 hour or until top is browned and cracked. The bread will sound hollow and will be quite firm to the touch.

Remove from the oven and cool for 10 minutes. Remove from tin and peel off baking paper. Refrigerate bread in an airtight container. The bread will keep for 1 week.

Great toasted!

Omit the sunflower seeds if they cause you problems.

Light White Bread

Makes 1 Loaf

250 g (2 ½ cups) almond flour
1 tsp baking soda
¼ tsp salt
3 eggs - separated
250 g (1 cup) scd yogurt^
1 Tbs honey

Preheat oven to 150°C/300°F
Line a 10 x 21 cm/4 x 8 inch loaf tin with baking paper

In a large bowl, mix the almond flour, baking soda and salt. Whisk the egg yolks with the yogurt^ and honey until light and fluffy. Beat the egg whites until stiff. Combine the egg yolk mixture with the almond flour until smooth. Add the stiff egg whites and gently blend. Pour the mixture into the prepared loaf tin and bake for 50- 60 minutes or until the top feels spongy. Let cool before slicing. Refrigerate in an airtight container.

This is a soft and fluffy bread and is great with savory toppings as well as sweet toppings.

It is too soft for the toaster, but will toast nicely under the grill.

Photo: Light White Bread

Pumpkin and Almond Bread

Makes 1 Loaf

400 g (4 cups) almond flour
1 tsp baking soda
½ tsp salt
3 eggs
60 g (¼ cup) butter - softened
200 g (1 cup) fresh pumpkin - cooked,
mashed
60 g (½ cup) walnuts - chopped
1 Tbs orange rind - grated
½ tsp ground ginger

Preheat the oven to 150°C/300°F
Line a 10 x 21 cm/4 x 8 inch loaf tin with baking paper

Combine the almond flour with the baking soda and salt. In another bowl whisk the eggs with the butter and add the pumpkin, walnuts, orange rind, and ginger. Combine the almond flour with the egg mixture until smooth. Pour the dough into the prepared loaf tin and bake for 1 hour, until the top of the loaf feels firm. Remove from oven and cool completely. Store in the refrigerator.

Cinnamon and Raisin Loaf

Makes 1 Loaf

350 g (3 ½ cups) almond flour
¼ tsp salt
1 tsp baking soda
3 eggs
250 g (1 cup) scd yogurt^
225 g (¾ cup) honey
100 g (½ cup) raisins
1 Tbs cinnamon
1 Tbs honey

Preheat oven to 150°C/300°F
Line a 10 x 21 cm/4 x 8 inch loaf tin with baking paper

Combine the almond flour, salt and baking soda. In another bowl, whisk the egg with the yogurt^ and honey. Mix the almond flour mixture with the egg mixture and raisins until well combined. Then in a small bowl mix the cinnamon with the 1 Tbs of honey. Pour the dough into the prepared loaf tin. With a flat butter knife, fold the honey/cinnamon mixture under the dough in big swirls. Bake for 1 ½ hours, or until the centre of the loaf feels spongy. Remove from the oven and let cool for 10 minutes before removing from the tin. Refrigerate in an airtight container.

Pumpkin and Sage Scones

Makes 8

2 eggs
2 Tbs honey
30 g butter - cold, diced small
150 g (1 cup) fresh pumpkin - cooked, mashed
½ tsp dried sage
300 g (3 cups) almond flour
1 tsp baking soda
¼ tsp salt

Preheat the grill to 150°C/300°F
Line a baking tray with baking paper.

Whisk the eggs and honey until light and fluffy. Mix in the butter, pumpkin, and sage. Combine the almond flour with the baking soda and salt and knead together with the egg mixture. Do not worry if there are little chunks of butter showing. Place large dollops, about 1 Tbs, of the dough onto the prepared baking tray and bake for about 30-40 minutes, until the scones are lightly browned and feel firm to the touch.

Crusty Onion Rolls

Makes 6

300 g (3 cups) almond flour
1 tsp baking soda
110 g (1 cup) cheddar - grated
1 tsp salt
1 tsp ground pepper
35 g (⅓ cup) onions - finely chopped
60 g (¼ cup) butter - softened
2 Tbs honey
2 eggs
olive oil

Preheat oven to 170°C/330°F
Line a baking tray with baking paper

Combine the almond flour with the baking soda, cheddar, salt, pepper, and onions. In another bowl, whisk the butter with the honey and eggs until frothy. Add the almond flour mixture to the egg mixture and knead together. With slightly moist hands, form the dough into 6 buns and place onto the lined baking tray. Trace a cross across the top of the rolls with a sharp knife and brush with oil. Place a heatproof dish with water into the bottom of the oven (this will make the rolls nice and crusty). Bake for about 15 minutes, then turn oven down to 150°C/300°F and bake for another 15 minutes. The rolls should feel firm and be nicely browned. Take out of the oven and let cool. Refrigerate in an airtight container.

Soft Soufflé Bread

Makes 6 slices

6 egg whites
pinch salt
4 egg yolks
100 g (3 oz) scd dripped yogurt^

Preheat oven to 150˚C/300˚F
Line a 22 x 33 cm/9 x 13 inch glass Pyrex dish with baking paper

Whip the egg whites and salt until stiff. Combine the egg yolks with the dripped yogurt^ and mix until smooth, then gently fold under the egg whites. Pour into the prepared Pyrex dish and bake for 30 minutes. Remove from the oven. Place another piece of baking paper onto a flat cutting board and tip the Pyrex dish with the dough onto the cutting board. Remove the baking paper from the underside of the bread and lift the bread with the new baking paper back into the Pyrex dish. Bake the bread for another 10 – 15 minutes. Let cool and store in a covered container in the refrigerator. This bread will toast nicely.

Breakfast

Baked Beans

Serves 8

400 g (2 cups) dried navy beans
2 Tbs olive oil
160 g (2 cups) onion – chopped
1 clove garlic – minced
680 ml (2 ¾ cups) tomato puree*
150 g (½ cup) honey
2 Tbs cider vinegar
¼ tsp ground nutmeg
¼ tsp ground cinnamon
3 bay leaves
¼ tsp ground black pepper
½ tsp ground turmeric
½ tsp ground cumin

*see page152 for recipe

Preheat oven to 150°C/300°F

Soak the beans overnight. Drain and rinse under cold water. Cook beans in boiling water for up to 2 hours. Drain beans and place into a large casserole dish. Heat the oil in a small skillet and sauté the onions and garlic until browned. Add the onions and garlic to the beans. Add all the other ingredients and stir. With the lid on, bake the beans for 3 ½ hours, stirring frequently. Check moisture level and add water if needed. After 3 ½ hours remove the cover and keep baking for another 30 minutes.

Refrigerate in an airtight jar for up to one week.

Breakfast Muffins

Makes 6

1 whole egg
2 eggs – separated
60 g (¼ cup) butter – softened
60 g (¼ cup) scd yogurt^
1 tsp honey
¼ tsp salt
50 g (½ cup) cheddar – grated
250 g (2 ½ cups) almond flour
1 tsp baking soda
2 hard-boiled eggs – peeled

Preheat oven to 150°C/300°F
Lightly oil a large 6-hole muffin tin

Combine the whole egg with the egg yolks, butter, yogurt^, honey and salt and whisk until light and fluffy. Add the grated cheddar and combine well. Mix the almond flour with the baking soda and combine with the egg mixture. Beat the two egg whites until stiff and gently fold into the dough. Chop the hard-boiled eggs into large chunks and fold into the mixture. Evenly distribute the dough into the muffin tin and bake for 40 minutes until the muffins feel spongy. Let cool for 10 minutes before serving warm with some butter.

Photo: Baked Beans and Breakfast Muffins

Scrambled Eggs

Serves 4

8 eggs
1 clove garlic - minced
2 Tbs scd french cream^
1 Tbs olive oil
salt and pepper to taste
several chives - chopped

Combine all ingredients and whisk until frothy. Reserve chopped chives for garnish. In a large skillet, heat the olive oil over medium heat. Add the egg mixture. Leave to cook for a minute before stirring with a wooden spoon. Slowly keep turning the egg mixture with the wooden spoon, breaking up the egg. Turn the heat off before most of the moisture has evaporated. The scrambled eggs should look slightly moist.

Serve decorated with the chopped chives on our toasted pumpernickel bread.

Banana Pikelets

Serves 4

5 eggs
1Tbs scd yogurt^
2 ripe bananas - sliced
1 Tbs honey

Add the eggs into a bowl and mix with the honey and yogurt^ until light and fluffy. Place oiled egg rings into a lightly greased non-stick pan. Heat the pan on high until it is hot and then reduce the heat. Slowly pour the mixture into the egg rings. Place three slices of banana on each pikelet. Fry on low heat until the egg starts to firm up. Turn pikelets and fry until golden brown. Serve with sliced banana and french cream. Drizzle with honey.

Pancakes

Serves 4

3 eggs
1 Tbs scd yogurt^
1 Tbs honey
100 g (1 cup) almond flour
½ tsp baking soda

Beat eggs, yogurt^, and honey until light and fluffy. Add almond flour and baking soda and stir until well combined. Heat a non-stick pan with a little oil. Pour in ⅓ **cup** of batter into the pan and fry until bubbles appear and the underside is golden brown. Flip and brown the other side. Serve warm with scd yogurt and our stewed apples or butter and honey.

Good Morning Breakfast Bars

300 g (1 cup) honey
35g (⅓ cup) butter
160 g (1 cup) mixed nuts*
60 g (1 cup) shredded coconut*
90 g (½ cup) pitted dates - chopped*
90 g (½ cup) pitted prunes - chopped*
90 g (½ cup) dried apricots - chopped*
1 tsp vanilla essence*

*see essential ingredients list

Preheat oven to 180°C/360°F.

Line a 20 cm (8 inch) square cake tin with baking paper.

Heat honey and butter in a saucepan, stir until butter has melted and is well combined with the honey. Turn off the heat and add all the other ingredients. Mix well and pour into the prepared cake tin. Bake for 30 minutes. Cool in refrigerator until set. Cut into bars and store between baking paper in an airtight container in refrigerator.

These bars need to be eaten straight from the refrigerator as they soften too much with warmer temperatures.

Muesli, Pears and Banana Whip

Makes 1 kg (2 lb)

Muesli
85 g (1 cup) flaked almonds
40 g (1 cup) flaked coconut*
45 g (½ cup) raisins
120 g (1 cup) pecans
65 g (½ cup) pine nuts
120 g (1 cup) dried apricots*
200 g (1 cup) prunes*

*see essential ingredients list

Serves 4

Topping
2 pears
1 tsp lemon juice
1 tsp honey

Banana Whip
250 ml (1 cup) scd yogurt^
1 ripe banana
1 Tbs honey

Place pecans, pine nuts, apricots, and prunes into a food processor and chop for about 5 - 10 seconds until roughly chopped. Remove into a bowl and mix with the almonds, coconut, and raisins. Store in an airtight container.

Peel and slice the pears and place into a saucepan with the lemon juice and honey. Cook, covered on low for about 10 minutes or until pears are just soft. Let them cool.

Blend the yogurt^, banana, and honey in a blender until smooth.

To serve, take ¼ cup of the banana yogurt and pour into a bowl. Top with 3 tablespoons of the muesli and 2 tablespoons of the pear. If desired, drizzle some extra honey over the top and serve.

Photo: Good Morning Breakfast Bar

Sun-Dried Tomato and Havarti Omelet

Makes 2 omelets

4 eggs
1 Tbs scd french cream^
1 clove garlic - minced
salt and pepper
2 egg whites
70 g (2 oz) sun-dried tomatoes -sliced
70 g (2 oz) havarti - sliced

Mix the eggs with the french cream^, garlic, salt and pepper and whisk until light and fluffy. Whisk the egg whites until stiff, and fold under the rest of the egg.

Heat a non-stick saucepan with a little oil. Pour in half the egg mixture, swishing it around to leave a thin layer of egg on the sides of the pan. Cook on medium heat for a few minutes. When the egg is 70% cooked swish again to distribute any uncooked egg evenly. Now add half the slivered sun-dried tomato and sliced havarti on top of one side of the omelet. With a spatula, flip the other side on top of the filling. Cook for a few more minutes. Place the omelet aside and keep warm. Repeat the process for the other omelet.

This omelet can be made with any fillings desired and tastes great with our sweet chili sauce.

Salmon Eggs Benedict

Serves 4

1 salmon fillet
olive oil
450 g (5 cups) spinach - chopped
1 Tbs white wine vinegar
4 eggs
cracked black pepper

In a small pan with some olive oil, fry the salmon for about 4 minutes on each side until cooked just through. Keep warm in the oven on minimal heat. Steam the spinach and place in the oven with the salmon to keep warm. Fill a medium size skillet halfway with water and add the vinegar. Heat the water until simmering. Keep simmering and crack the eggs into the pan, being careful not to break the yolk. Alternatively, use an egg poacher, which makes life very easy. Eggs are done when the whites have become solid.

Place a quarter of the spinach onto a plate, layer some of the salmon on top, and then place the poached egg on top of the salmon. Serve with hollandaise sauce and sprinkle on cracked black pepper.

Hollandaise Sauce

Serves 4

3 egg yolks
2 Tbs water
175 g (6 oz) unsalted butter - cubed
2 Tbs fresh lemon juice
salt and pepper

Place a heatproof bowl on top of a saucepan filled a quarter of the way up with water. Do not let the water boil, but keep it at a simmer. Place the egg yolks and water into the bowl and whisk for about 3 minutes until the mixture becomes quite thick and has doubled in volume. Add the butter a cube at a time, waiting until the previous cube has melted completely. This will take about 10 minutes. Keep whisking until the sauce starts to thicken. Remove from heat. Whisk in the lemon juice and season with salt and pepper. An electric whisk will take the pressure off your arm and the cooking time will be reduced by about half. Serve immediately.

Photo: Salmon Eggs Benedict

Warm Seasonal Fruit with Vanilla Yogurt

Serves 4

2 pears - peeled, chopped
2 Granny Smith apples - peeled, sliced
2 ripe bananas - sliced
1 kiwi fruit - peeled, sliced
8 strawberries - hulled, sliced
120 ml (½ cup) fresh orange juice
1 Tbs fresh lime juice
2 Tbs honey
1 tsp vanilla essence*

Topping
250 g (1 cup) scd yogurt^
1 tsp vanilla essence*
honey to taste

*see essential ingredients list

Heat the orange juice in a large skillet and add the pears, apples, lime juice, honey, vanilla essence, and sauté covered for 3 minutes. Add the banana, kiwi fruit and strawberries and cook covered for 1 minute. With a slotted spoon lift the fruit out of the skillet, draining off the orange juice and place into individual bowls.

Whisk together the yogurt^, vanilla, honey, and pour over the warmed fruit. Serve warm.

Beverages

Every Morning Smoothie

Serves 2

500 g (2 cups) scd yogurt^
1 ripe banana - chopped
70 g (½ cup) frozen berries
2 Tbs honey

Pour yogurt^, banana, berries, and honey into a blender and process for 1 minute. Pour into large glasses and serve immediately.

Flu Fighter

Makes 4 cups

1 ½ ltr (6 cups) water
80 ml (⅓ cup) fresh lemon juice
3 cloves garlic - peeled, bruised
3 Tbs fresh ginger - peeled,
roughly chopped
¼ tsp cayenne
3 tsp (or 3 bags) green tea
150 g (½ cup) honey

Place all the ingredients except for the honey into a pot with the water and bring to boil. Turn down heat and simmer for 40 minutes, or until half the liquid has evaporated. Take off the heat and add the honey to the mixture. Drink hot. Can be reheated when needed.

Almond Milk

Makes 500 ml (2 cups)

150 g (1 ½ cups) almond flour
750 ml (3 cups) water

Combine almond flour and water in a food processor and process for 3 minutes. Line a sieve with 4 kitchen cloths and pour in the almond mixture. Let drain, squeezing out as much milk as possible.

Refrigerate.

Lemonade

Makes about 4 liters (16 cups)

300 g (1 cup) honey
250 ml (1 cup) water
juice from 6 lemons
3 ½ liters (14 cups) of water

Heat the honey and 250ml/1 cup water in a large pot until the honey is well combined with the water. Let cool and add the lemon juice. Add the rest of the water and keep in airtight bottles in the refrigerator. If concentrated lemon cordial is desired, only add 1 liter/4 cup of water after boiling. Serve over ice, diluting the cordial to the desired strength.

Morning Perk

Makes 1 liter (4 cups)

500 ml (2 cups) fresh orange juice
500 ml (2 cups) water
2 black teabags
1 tsp whole cloves
1 stick cinnamon
honey to taste

Strain the orange juice to remove any pulp. Pour into a medium sized saucepan and add the water. Add all other ingredients and bring to boil. Boil for 5 minutes, then let sit for another 5 minutes. Strain the tea and add honey to taste.

After Dinner Spiced Tea

Makes 1 liter (4 cups)

2 Tbs ginger - roughly chopped
2 cinnamon sticks
2 tsp cardamom seeds - crushed
2 tsp fennel seeds - whole
1 ¼ ltr (5 cups) water
honey to taste

Place all the ingredients except honey into a pot with the water and bring to boil. Turn down heat and simmer for 20 minutes. Serve hot sweetened to taste with honey.

Photo: Lemonade

Raspberry Cordial

Makes 1 Liter (4 cups)

500 g frozen raspberries
300 g (1 cup) honey
2 lemons – juice only
1 ltr (4 cups) boiling water

Place the raspberries and honey into a medium size saucepan. Heat slowly and cook covered for 15 – 20 minutes until fruit has released all its juices. Let cool, then line a large sieve with four layers of cheesecloth and strain the juice, squeezing the cloth gently until all the juice has been extracted. Discard the pulp. Juice the lemons and strain them into the cordial. Add boiling water to the mixture. Bottle and refrigerate. To make a delicious iced drink, place some ice into a large glass, add ¼ cup of cordial and fill with cold water.

Iced Tea

Makes 250ml (1 cup)

60 ml (¼ cup) chai syrup (see below)
180 ml (¾ cup) cold water
sliced lemon
Ice

Place some ice into a glass, add our chai syrup and fill with cold water. Stir and serve with a slice of lemon.

Chai Syrup

Makes 1 Liter (4 cups)

2 liters (8 cups) water
300 g (1 cup) honey
3 cinnamon sticks
12 cardamom pods – bruised
12 whole cloves
12 whole black peppercorns
6 tsp black leaf tea

Place all the ingredients into a pot with the water and bring to boil. Turn down heat and simmer for 20 minutes. Serve hot - sweetened with honey to taste.

The syrup is used diluted 1:4 in iced tea or hot tea.

Chai Tea

Makes 250ml (1 cup)

60 ml (¼ cup) chai syrup
180 ml (¾ cup) hot water
sliced lemon

Pour the syrup and hot water into a mug and add the lemon slices. Enjoy!

Index

Numbers in **bold** indicate photographs

I also want to thank Randolph Lagerway for his patience and passion for this project, as without him and his skillful staff this book would not have come off the ground as fast as it did. His website design, marketing skills and creative way with words are outstanding and have given the book an all over professional polish. I look forward to working with Randy and his team at Force 8 well into the future.

Acknowledgements

First of all, I would like to thank **Elaine Gottschall** for bringing this diet to the attention of the world. And to her daughter, **Judy Herod** for continuing the legacy. Thank-you Judy for your encouragement with this endeavor.

Carol Frilegh (celiac). A long-time veteran of the SCDiet and a close friend of Elaine's, your passionate support of this cookbook has been extremely inspirational. Your meticulous scrutiny of the recipes and ingredients has ensured compliance of the book with the diet. Thank-you Carol!

Thanks also to **Matthew Jackson**, the dedicated moderator of SCDOZ — the Australian & New Zealand internet support group for the Specific Carbohydrate Diet. Your expert vetting of the recipes also ensured consistency with the SCDiet. Thank-you for your kind words of support.

Sheila Trenholm (ulcerative colitis). Thank-you for finding the time in your hectic schedule as a full time mom to give me your expert input on the foods used in the book. As a 6 year veteran of the diet, and a degree holder in biology with an extensive background in testing food products, your involvement helps cement our confidence in the book being 100% SCDiet compliant.

Pamela J. Ferro, (mother of child with autism) RN President of Hopewell Associates and founder of the Gottschall Autism Center in Massachussetts. Pam, your encouragement throughout the development of the book motivated me to press on. I am delighted to be able to return that support with a donation from each book sold.

Ronald L. Hoffman, MD. of the Hoffman Center, New York. Thank-you for your eloquent and extremely poignant foreword which introduces this book. Your involvement with Elaine Gottschall and her book *Breaking The Vicious Cycle* 14 years ago makes you a leader among practicing specialists in the field of intestinal health. Lending your name to this book does me a great honor.

References

Canada
Lucy's Kitchen Shop
www.LucysKitchenShop.com
Yoghurt Starter
Acidophilus Capsules
Frozen Dessert Maker
Food Dehydrator
Almond Flour
Books

Almond Flour
John Vince Store
416-636-6146 EXT #1 (Code #13009)

Grain-Free JK Gourmet is a Canadian company devoted to making all-natural, preservative-free baked goods of outstanding flavour and quality. http://www.jkgourmet.ca/

Australia
SCD legal Dry Curd Cottage Cheese
Premier Dairies 102-104 Ballandella Road Pendle Hill NSW 2145, ph 02 9631 3166

Almond Meal/Flour
AlmondCo
Telephone: 61 8 8595 1770   Facsimile: 61 8 8595 1559   www.almondco.com.au/

Sausage Maker
All Food Equipment
Ph: (02) 9896 3300 www.allfoodequipment.com.au

USA
SCD Bakery   Wide range of SCD compliant baked goods
www.SCDbakery.com

Almond Flour Suppliers
http://www.almondsarein.com/AlmondLovers/content.cfm?ItemNumber=1585

UK
Well Hung Meat   Pure meat sausages
www.wellhungmeat.com   0845 230 3131

Nut Flour and Dried Fruits
HBS Foods Limited
Tel. 01384 457705   www.hbsfoods.co.uk

The Flour Bin
Suppliers of nut flour
www.flourbin.com   01246 850124

(Visit our website for many more supplier references: www.CCCCIBS.com)

Special Offer to Readers...

I would like to give you a special thank-you for purchasing this book. Simply visit **www.CCCCIBS.com/reader** to receive a special offer.

If you haven't already seen the website, it is packed with valuable information for those suffering with intestinal problems, focusing on the Specific Carbohydrate Diet.

Information includes:
- Links to associations, discussion forums, and specialist IBD related websites.
- SCDiet related websites around the world
- Links to other SCD books
- Descriptions of intestinal diseases and relation to the SCDiet.
- Links to latest relevant medical research news.
- Forum to share questions and suggestions with like-minded people
- Author's personal Food Log (FLOG!)
- Special offers

www.ccccibs.com

Quick Conversion Guide

Wherever you live in the world, you can use our recipes with the help of our easy-to-follow conversions for all your cooking needs. These conversions are approximate only. The difference between the exact and approximate conversions of liquid and dry measures amounts to only a teaspoon or two, and will not make any difference to your cooking results.

Measuring Equipment
The difference between measuring cups internationally is minimal within 2 or 3 teaspoons' difference (For the record, 1 Australian metric measuring cup will hold approximately 250ml). The most accurate way of measuring dry ingredients is to weigh them. When measuring liquids use a clear glass or plastic jug with metric markings.

NOTE: NZ, CANADA, USA AND UK ALL USE 15 ml TABLESPOONS. ALL CUP AND SPOON MEASUREMENTS ARE LEVEL.

DRY MEASURES

Metric	Imperial
15 g	1/2 oz
30 g	1 oz
60 g	2 oz
90 g	3 oz
125 g	4 oz (¼ lb)
155 g	5 oz
185 g	6 oz
220 g	7 oz
250 g	8 oz (½ lb)
280 g	9 oz
315 g	10 oz
345 g	11 oz
375 g	12 oz (¾ lb)
410 g	13 oz
440 g	14 oz
470 g	15 oz
500 g	16 oz (¾ lb)
750 g	24 oz (1 ½ lb)
1 kg	32 oz (2 lb)

LIQUID MEASURES

Metric	Imperial
30 ml	1 fl. oz
60 ml	2 fl. oz
100 ml	3 fl. oz
125 ml	4 fl. oz
150 ml	5 fl. oz (¼ pint)
190 ml	6 fl. oz
250 ml	8 fl. oz
300 ml	10 fl. oz (½ pint)
500 ml	16 fl. oz
600 ml	20 fl. oz (1 pint)
(1 Litre)1000 ml	1 ¾ pints

fl. oz	fluid ounce
g	gram
lb	pound
ltr	liter
ml	milliliter
oz	ounce
Tbs	Tablespoon
tsp	teaspoon

OVEN TEMPERATURES

These oven temperatures are only a guide; we have given you the lower degree of heat. Always check the manufacturer's manual.

C° (Celsius)	F° (Fahrenheit)	Gas Mark
120	250	1
150	300	2
160	325	3
180	350	4
190	375	5
200	400	6
230	450	7

We use large eggs with an average weight of 60g.